Kid's Box

Teacher's Resource Book 3

with Online Audio

Second Edition

Kathryn Escribano with Caroline Nixon & Michael Tomlinson

CAMBRIDGE
UNIVERSITY PRESS

CAMBRIDGE
UNIVERSITY PRESS

University Printing House, Cambridge CB2 8BS, United Kingdom

Cambridge University Press is part of the University of Cambridge.

It furthers the University's mission by disseminating knowledge in the pursuit of education, learning and research at the highest international levels of excellence.

www.cambridge.org
Information on this title: www.cambridge.org/9780110766474

First published 2008
Second edition 2015

Printed in Poland by Opolgraf

A catalogue record for this publication is available from the British Library

ISBN 978-1-107-66647-4 Teacher's Resource Book with Online Audio 3
ISBN 978-1-107-65450-1 Pupil's Book 3
ISBN 978-1-107-64400-7 Activity Book with Online Resources 3
ISBN 978-1-107-65248-4 Teacher's Book 3
ISBN 978-1-107-65464-8 Class Audio CDs 3 (3 CDs)
ISBN 978-1-107-67585-8 Flashcards 3 (pack of 109)
ISBN 978-1-107-69691-4 Interactive DVD with Teacher's Booklet 3
ISBN 978-1-107-43187-4 Presentation Plus 3
ISBN 978-1-107-64380-2 Language Portfolio 3
ISBN-978-1-107-61895-4 Posters 3
ISBN 978-1-107-61806-0 Tests CD-ROM and Audio CD 3-4

Additional resources for this publication at www.cambridge.org/kidsbox

Contents

Introduction 4

Teacher's notes and worksheets

Hello! 8

Unit 1: Family matters 15

Unit 2: Home sweet home 22

Unit 3: A day in the life 29

Unit 4: In the city 36

Unit 5: Fit and well 43

Unit 6: A day in the country 50

Unit 7: World of animals 57

Unit 8: Weather report 64

Festivals 71

Word cards 80

Tests

Test Units 1–4 90

Test Units 5–8 113

Test key and tapescript 137

Diploma 143

Introduction

- This Teacher's Resource Book is designed to help you and your pupils make the most of *Kid's Box 3* as well as providing practice for the Cambridge English: Young Learners (YLE) Tests. There are three main sections in this Pack:
  - Worksheets
  - Word cards
  - Practice tests

Worksheets

- There are two reinforcement worksheets and two extension worksheets per unit. The former are designed for revision and to help those pupils who need extra practice whilst the latter are designed to cater for the needs of fast finishers. However, these worksheets not only provide a resource for mixed-ability classes but also offer material to set as homework or for the rest of the class to use while you work individually with a pupil on a speaking test.

- Reinforcement worksheet 1 for each unit focuses on key vocabulary, whilst reinforcement worksheet 2 provides further practice of the structures. Extension worksheet 1 is more challenging. It is designed for fast finishers who need a more cognitively demanding type of activity. Extension worksheet 2 offers further exploitation of the unit story.

- There is also a song worksheet for each unit. These always give the song lyrics and a song-based activity which varies from unit to unit. These worksheets are best done once pupils are familiar with the song. The songs are provided online on the *Kid's Box* website but you can also use the Class Audio CDs. Please note that the track numbers refer to *Kid's Box 3 Online Audio*.

- Finally, each unit has a content-based topic worksheet. As explained in the Teacher's Book, the content-based lessons in the Pupil's Book and Activity Book aim to teach and reinforce understanding of subject topics which pupils learn in their other classes, through the medium of English. Thus, there is a dual aim: that of learning subject content and learning language. The topic worksheets in this Resource Book add to and go beyond the content-based pages in the Pupil's Book and Activity Book.

- There is a page of teaching notes before the worksheets for each unit. These notes include optional follow-up activities which encourage interaction between pupils and add a useful dimension to the worksheet. You may find that one type of follow-up activity works better than another with your particular class, in which case you can use the suggestions as a springboard for adapting other worksheets.

- You may find, according to the particular interests of a pupil, that in one unit, he/she needs a reinforcement worksheet whilst in other units, or at other times, the same pupil can more profitably do an extension worksheet. Fast finishers may want/need to do reinforcement and extension worksheets.

- You can also use the worksheets as gap-fillers or alternative activities when, for example, some other activity has interfered with the normal running of the class.

- The worksheets can also be used as models for you or your pupils to develop further practice activities. Creating exercises is an excellent way for pupils to consolidate their learning and they will enjoy swapping them with their friends.

- You may find it useful to keep a record of the worksheets each pupil has completed.

- After the resources for each unit, there are two worksheets for each of the following festivals:
  - Halloween
  - Christmas
  - Easter

- The teaching notes for this section contain cultural notes on the festivals which you can use to introduce the topics to the class.

Word cards

- For each unit, there are photocopiable word cards with the key vocabulary items of each unit. These are to support you in the introduction and consolidation of literacy in English in the classroom. You may wish to mount the photocopied words on card and laminate them so that they can be used over and over again. You may also like to enlarge them on a photocopier before doing so.

- Some ideas for using the word cards:
  - Display them in the classroom so that the 'walls talk'.
  - Give photocopies to the pupils to make into dictionaries.
  - Use them for rhyme practice, asking pupils to select two that sound the same or one that has the same sound as the word you say.
  - Reveal one letter at a time, asking pupils to spell out the word or guess it.
  - Make them into card games.
  - Use them as prompts when asking pupils to write and speak.

- It is easy to put away one set of word cards as you move on to a new unit, but remember that it is very useful to mix them in with subsequent vocabulary sets. You can use them to recycle and test vocabulary throughout the year.

Practice tests

- There are two progress tests, each covering four units. The tests are suitable for all classes as they review the vocabulary and structures of the preceding units. In addition, they offer specific practice for the Movers level of the Cambridge English: Young Learners (YLE) Tests. It should be remembered, however, that much of the YLE Movers Test uses texts in the past tense. Clearly, at this stage, the practice tests cannot reflect this reality. Therefore, the focus here is on the various activity types and the test format. The more familiar the pupils are with these, the more confidence they will have when they do the YLE Movers Test having completed *Kid's Box 4*.

YLE activity types in *Kid's Box 3* tests

Task	Approximate duration	Expected response	Tips
Listening	25 minutes		Ensure pupils know that each listening text is heard twice. Encourage them to listen to the complete recording before answering questions.
Listen and draw lines.		Draw lines to match names to people in a picture.	Ensure that pupils realise there is one extra name at the top or bottom of the page which will not be mentioned. Make sure the pupils know which first names are male and which are female, and which can be both: *Alex, Kim, Pat* and *Sam*. Warn them not to jump to conclusions. They must listen to all the information.
Listen and write.		Write words or numbers in gaps.	Practise by doing similar productive tasks in the classroom. Encourage pupils to be as accurate as possible in their spelling, though some misspellings will be allowed for words not spelt out on the recording. Ensure that pupils realise they have to write responses which make sense, given the prompts.
Listen and draw a line from the day to the correct picture.		Draw lines from days of week to correct pictures.	Encourage pupils to draw a line to the appropriate picture in the most direct way possible. Make sure they know each day is only used once and one day will not be used at all. Encourage pupils not to leave questions unanswered. Once they have used the days they are sure about, they should make an intelligent guess about the remaining pictures.
Listen and tick the box.		Tick boxes under correct pictures.	Ensure that the pupils listen to the whole dialogue before deciding on their answer. Recycle vocabulary throughout.
Listen and colour and draw or write.		Carry out instructions to colour and draw or write.	Practise colour vocabulary (black, blue, brown, green, grey, orange, pink, purple, red, yellow). Remind pupils that they will either have to draw or write something for one of the questions. Train pupils to listen carefully for prepositional phrases which describe exactly where something is.

Task	Approximate duration	Expected response	Tips
Reading and writing	30 minutes		**Correct spelling is required in all parts of the Reading and Writing Test.** Encourage pupils to write clearly. It is often better not to use joined-up writing. Train pupils to write only as much as they need to. Give time limits when doing classroom tasks, to help pupils learn time management. Make sure pupils are familiar with the structures and words in the Starters and Movers syllabuses.
Look and read. Choose the correct words and write them on the lines.		Copy correct words next to definitions.	Give pupils practice in reading and writing definitions. Give pupils practice in accurate copying. Remind pupils to copy the whole option and not to add anything extra. Train pupils to correct their spelling.
Look and read. Write 'yes' or 'no'.		Write 'yes' or 'no'.	Give pupils practice in matching sentences to pictures. Remind pupils that the sentence must be completely true according to the picture for a 'yes' answer.
Read the text and choose the best answer.		Choose the correct response by circling a letter.	Remind pupils to read all the options before choosing the correct one. Practise appropriate responses, not just to questions, but also to statements. Give pupils practice with the use of set expressions and with short 'yes'/'no' answers. Give pupils practice with multiple-choice questions.
Read the story. Write one-word answers.		Choose and copy missing words correctly. Tick a box to choose the best title for the story.	Encourage pupils to read holistically for a sense of the text before trying to fill the first gap. Train pupils to read the text surrounding the question to be able to correctly fill the gap. Give pupils practice in guessing which word could go into a gap. Practise choosing the right form of words within sentences and texts. Help pupils to identify words or structures that indicate what form of word the answer should be.
Look at the pictures and read the story. Answer the questions.		Complete sentences about a story by writing 1, 2 or 3 words.	**Pupils must not write more than three words.** Train pupils to predict an outline of the story from the three pictures and the title. Practise reading for gist. Practise understanding whole texts by selecting titles for paragraphs or complete stories. Practise finding synonyms for nouns, identifying what is being referred to in a text, using pronouns to replace nouns and turning sentences around without altering the meaning. Ensure that words chosen to complete sentences are grammatically correct.
Read the text. Choose the right words and write them on the lines.		Complete a text by selecting the correct words and copying them in the corresponding gaps.	Practise choosing and forming the correct type of word to fit into sentences and texts. Remind pupils to choose from the three options given. Practise general reading skills.

Task	Approximate duration	Expected response	Tips
Speaking	5–7 minutes		The mark is based on ratings for interactive listening ability, production of extended responses and pronunciation. Pupils are required to follow simple instructions and talk about different pictures, and to answer simple questions about themselves.
Describe two pictures by using short responses.		Identify four differences between pictures.	Give pupils practice in describing differences between two similar pictures.
Understand the beginning of a story and then continue it based on a series of pictures.		Describe each picture in turn.	Give pupils practice in telling simple picture stories. Practise using *There is/are*, the present tense of the verbs *be* and *have (got)*, the modals *can/can't* and *must/mustn't* and the present continuous.
Suggest a picture which is different and explain why.		Identify the odd one out and give a reason.	Practise identifying the different one in a set of four pictures.
Understand and respond to personal questions.		Answer personal questions.	Give pupils practice in answering questions about themselves, their families and friends, their homes, their school and free-time activities, their likes and dislikes. Use English to give everyday classroom instructions. Make sure pupils are happy using *Hello, Goodbye* and *Thank you*, and that they have plenty of practice using *Sorry,* or *I don't understand.*

Reinforcement worksheet 1

- Pupils use the international flag code to decipher the names of the characters. They then look at the pictures and complete the sentences.

Key: 1 Sam – comics, 2 John – train, 3 Bill – football, 4 Jane – bike.

- *Optional follow-up activity:* Pupils use the code to write their own message. They then swap messages and decode them.

Reinforcement worksheet 2

- Pupils use the pictures to help them follow the letter trail in the word mazes from *In* to *Out*. They write the words below the pictures.

Key: 1 kite, 2 train, 3 camera, 4 bike, 5 doll, 6 helicopter, 7 lorry, 8 computer, 9 monster, 10 board game.

- *Optional follow-up activity:* Pupils draw an empty grid in their notebook to prepare a similar puzzle for a friend, using words they wish to revise.

Extension worksheet 1

- Pupils affix a photo of themselves (or draw themselves) and use the visual prompts to write sentences about what they can and can't do.

- *Optional follow-up activity:* In groups of four, each pupil asks the pupil on his/her left two *Can you … ?* questions based on the visual prompts. When all the questions have been asked, they take it in turns to recall what their partner can and can't do.

Extension worksheet 2

- This can be done as a listening exercise (Track 2) or a reading exercise. Pupils decide which sentence goes in each gap and then write the numbers in the boxes.

Key: See Pupil's Book, page 9.

- *Optional follow-up activity:* Pupils work in groups of four. Together they decide on four of the story frames and each pupil then cuts out these four frames. They then shuffle all the cards together and deal them out equally. They say *1, 2, 3, pass!* then discard one card face down in front of the player on their left. Each player picks up the new card and decides which card to discard next. The winner is the first player to end up with four cards the same.

Song worksheet

- Pupils listen to the song (Track 3) twice. The first time they fill in the gaps over the dotted lines using words from the top box; the second time they fill in the gaps over the solid lines using words from the second box.

Key: See Pupil's Book, page 7.

- *Optional follow-up activity:* Pupils colour the toys and write new lyrics for the song underneath.

Topic worksheet

- Pre-teach words you think the pupils may find difficult. Pupils read the text then invent their own legend. They can draw a comic strip or draw a strange animal and write a text like the one about the 'cabbit'.

- *Optional follow-up activity:* Pupils use an atlas or world map to locate the Isle of Man.

 **Hello!**

Reinforcement worksheet 1

 Find and write.

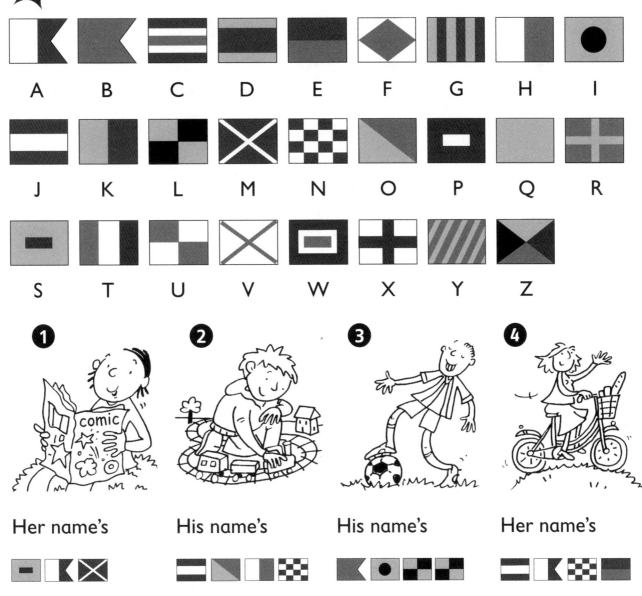

Her name's

S a m

His name's

_ _ _ _

His name's

_ _ _ _

Her name's

_ _ _ _

 Complete the sentences.

Number 1 is called Sam_____ . She likes reading comics_____ .

Number 2 is called _____ . He likes playing with his toy _____ .

Number 3 is called _____ . He likes playing _____ .

Number 4 is called _____ . She likes riding her _____ .

 © Cambridge University Press 2015   Kid's Box Teacher's Resource Book 3

Hello!

 # Reinforcement worksheet 2

 ## Look, follow and write.

1 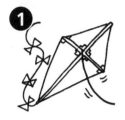 **2** **3** **4** **5**

kite_____   _____   _____   _____   _____

In ➡

k	c	r	e	y	i	q	c
l	t	i	g	m	e	e	v
e	e	u	b	a	r	u	b
l	t	r	n	c	a	d	o
s	l	a	i	h	b	e	l
a	m	f	w	p	i	k	l
b	i	j	x	s	u	t	r

➡ Out

6  **7**  **8**  **9**  **10**

_____   _____   _____   _____   _____

In ➡

h	i	c	e	y	i	o	n
e	l	o	g	m	r	m	s
e	t	p	b	t	e	e	t
l	e	z	n	u	a	r	b
l	r	a	m	p	r	a	o
o	y	c	o	p	d	m	e
r	r	j	x	s	g	a	r

➡ Out

Kid's Box Teacher's Resource Book 3   © Cambridge University Press 2015   **PHOTOCOPIABLE**

Hello! Extension worksheet 1

 Think and write.

This is me. I am _____ years old.

I can/can't _____ .

I _____ .

I _____ .

I _____ .

I _____ .

I _____ .

I _____ .

I _____ .

© Cambridge University Press 2015   Kid's Box Teacher's Resource Book 3

Hello! Extension worksheet 2

 Think and write.

Panel 1: Hello. This is the Lock and Key Detective Agency. Sorry we can't answer the phone at the moment. **1** ____

Panel 2: **2** ____ I'm in the house next to your agency. I can't find Clarence!

Panel 3: Argh! Oops! Hello, hello. This is Key. **3** ____

TRIP!

Panel 4: Oh! **4** ____ He's a big fat cat. **5** ____ **6** ____

Panel 5: Get the Detective Box, Key. **7** ____

Panel 6: Come on, Key. **8** ____

We're looking for a big white cat, Lock. No problem.

Please		Questions		Have got	
Please find Clarence.		What are we looking for?		We've got work to do!	
Please help me!		Can I help you?		He hasn't got a tail.	
Please leave a message.	1			He's got long white fur and blue eyes.	

Kid's Box Teacher's Resource Book 3 © Cambridge University Press 2015

PHOTOCOPIABLE

Hello! Song worksheet

 Listen and do. Sing.

| small | fat | ~~old~~ | big | new |

| driving | talking | riding | flying | bouncing | walking |

I've got an __old__ bike
And I'm _____ it.
He's got a _____ kite
And he's _____ it.
She's got a _____ car
And she's _____ it.
We've got toys!

I've got a _____ doll
And it's _____ .
He's got a robot
And it's _____ .
She's got a _____ ball
And it's _____ .
We've got toys!

She's got a black car
And she's driving it.

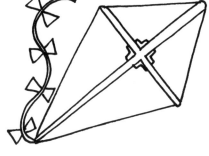

© Cambridge University Press 2015   Kid's Box Teacher's Resource Book 3

Hello! Topic worksheet

 Read and write.

Lock and Key are looking for a cat called Clarence. Clarence hasn't got a tail. There is a kind of cat called a Manx cat which hasn't got a tail.

This is a legend about the Manx cat:

The animals are in Noah's ark. The cat is playing outside.

It is raining. Noah is closing the door. The cat is running.

The door is closed. The cat is inside. His tail is outside. The cat hasn't got a tail.

What are Manx cats and where are they from?

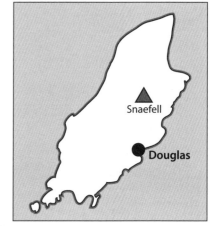

Manx cats have got long back legs and short front legs. Some people say the Manx cat is half cat and half rabbit. They call it a 'cabbit'!

Manx cats come from the Isle of Man. The Isle of Man is an island in the Irish Sea between England, Wales, Scotland and Ireland. The capital city is Douglas. There is a mountain on the island. It is called Snaefell.

The flag is red. On the flag there is a symbol called the Three Legs of Man. Can you see the legs running?

Kid's Box Teacher's Resource Book 3   © Cambridge University Press 2015

Reinforcement worksheet 1

- Pupils complete the two sentences, putting one letter on each dash. They then use these same letters to fill in the gaps in the second part of the exercise. Finally, they write the words in the correct columns. Make sure they understand the meaning of 'doing words/verbs' and 'describing words/adjectives'.

Key: granddaughter, grandson. Family: grandmother, uncle, aunt, grandparents, son, grandfather, brother, sister, daughter.
Doing words/verbs: shopping, going, reading, swimming, painting, riding.
Describing words/adjectives: clever, curly, quiet, straight, black, fair.

- *Optional follow-up activity:* In groups, pupils form sentences of their own using words from each column. One pupil begins the sentence and the next adds to it. When they cannot continue with the sentence, they start another one.

Reinforcement worksheet 2

- Make sure the pupils understand the key and can name all the actions. Ask them to focus on Jane and the way all the other characters are related to her. They write five sentences of their own about the characters' likes and dislikes.

Key: Jane's grandpa doesn't like swimming.
Jane's grandma loves playing the piano.
Jane's dad doesn't like running.
Jane's mum likes driving.
Jane's uncle loves football.
Jane's aunt doesn't like badminton.
Jane loves reading.
Jane's brother loves reading.
Jane's sister likes riding her bike.

- *Optional follow-up activity:* Pupils draw their own family tree with the likes and dislikes of the different family members and then swap them so that they can write sentences about their classmates' families.

Extension worksheet 1

- Pupils read the text and look at the picture to work out who each character is. They then describe each character's hair.

Key: Peter has got short black curly hair. Jane has got long black curly hair. Daisy has got long fair curly hair. Sally has got short straight black hair. Fred has got short straight black hair.

- *Optional follow-up activity:* Pupils count how many in the class have hair like Peter, Jane, etc. They then write sentences.

Extension worksheet 2

- This can be done as a listening exercise (Track 4) or a reading exercise. Pupils look at the negative sentences and phrases at the bottom of the page and make them affirmative. They then decide which frame each affirmative sentence belongs to.

Key: See Pupil's Book, page 15.

- *Optional follow-up activity:* Pupils work in groups of four. Each pupil cuts out the six frames. They then shuffle all the cards together and deal them out equally. Working in a clockwise direction, pupils take it in turns to place a card on the table. The card must be frame one or the next frame in a line (frame two goes after frame one, frame three after frame two, and so on). If a pupil cannot place a card, he/she must pass. The winner is the first player to get rid of all his/her cards.

Song worksheet

- Pupils listen to the song (Track 5) twice and decide which pair of song lines goes where. The first time they listen, they write the letter and the second time they check their answers. They then copy the lyrics onto the lines in the correct order.

Key: See Pupil's Book, page 13.

- *Optional follow-up activity:* Pupils work in groups. They take it in turns to sing/say one of the pairs of lines. The first person to sing/say the next pair of lines in the song has the next go.

Topic worksheet

- Pupils use the clues to help them re-write the three texts. Make sure they keep their Pupil's Books closed while they do this. They then choose one of the descriptions and draw their own version of the portrait. Encourage them to reflect the artist's style.

Key: See Pupil's Book, page 16.

- *Optional follow-up activity:* Pupils work in groups. They all put their pictures on the table and take it in turns to describe one. The others must guess which picture is being described.

Reinforcement worksheet 1

 Think and write.

I am Grandpa Star's

_ _ _ _ _ _ _ _ _ _ _ _ _ _ _ .

I am Grandma Star's

_ _ _ _ _ _ _ _ _ .

clev_r	ri_ing	cu_ly	_wimming
da_ghter	g_andmother	quie_	gran_father
shoppin_	p_inting	goin_	siste_
gra_dparents	brot_er	rea_ing	strai_ht
f_ir	s_n	u_cle	au_t
bl_ck			

Family	Doing words	Describing words
grandmother	....	....
....	....	....
....	....	....
....	....	....
....	....	....
....	....	....
....		
....		
....		

 Write sentences using words from each column.

Reinforcement worksheet 2

★ **Think and write.**

❤❤	loves
❤	likes
✗	doesn't like

Jane

Examples

Jane's grandpa doesn't like swimming.

Jane's grandma loves playing the piano.

Extension worksheet 1

★ **Read, think and write.**

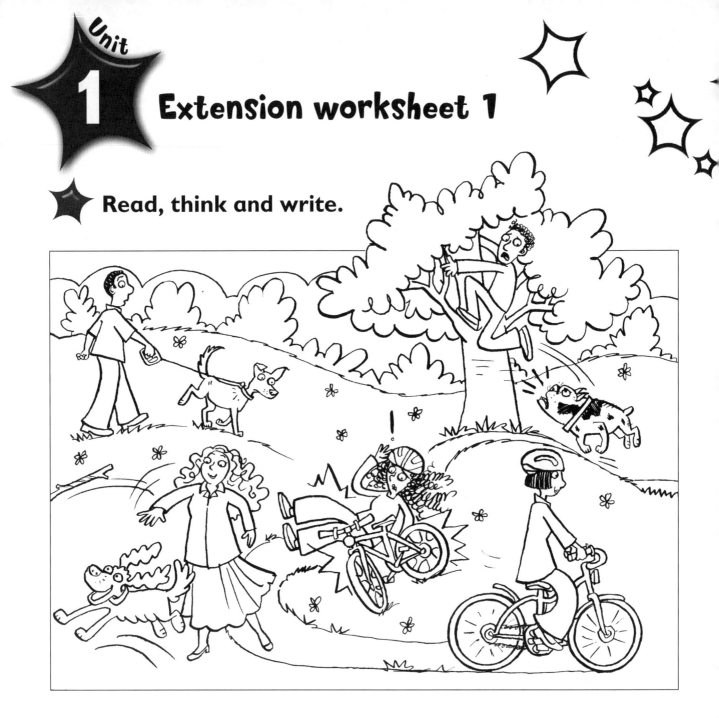

Five people are in the park. Their names are Peter, Jane, Daisy, Sally and Fred. Sally and Jane have got bikes but Jane can't ride her bike very well. Only Daisy and Fred like dogs.

Is their hair long or short, black or fair, curly or straight?

Peter has got short black curly hair   .

Jane   .

Daisy   .

Sally   .

Fred   .

Kid's Box Teacher's Resource Book 3   © Cambridge University Press 2015   **PHOTOCOPIABLE**

Extension worksheet 2

 04 **Change and write.**

Hmm, that's the pet thief. He's got straight black hair, a black beard and a moustache.

WANTED Pet Thief

Yes, and he's wearing a big dirty hat and an old jacket. **a** _____, no problem!

Where are you going, Lock?

b _____ find that pet thief. Let's look in the park.

c _____ There's the pet thief ... and he's got Clarence!

Yes, I can see his dirty hat and old jacket. Let's get him!

There you are Clarence! Naughty cat!

What are you doing? **d** _____ Who are you?

I'm Mr Key, from Lock and Key Detective Agency. We're looking for the pet thief.

I'm not a pet thief!

e _____, Key. She hasn't got a beard or a moustache. Give her the cat.

No problem, Lock.

1 Don't look! → *Look!* .... | c |

2 That's not right → .... | |

3 I don't want to → .... | |

4 Don't give me my cat! → .... | |

5 We can't find him → .... | |

1 Song worksheet

⭐ ▶05 **Listen and do. Sing.**

 a Grandpa Star is funny,
And his curly hair is grey.

~~c Aunt May's a doctor,~~
~~She's got straight black hair.~~

b Suzy isn't quiet,
But she's very small.

----

c Aunt May's a doctor,
She's got straight black hair.

----

d His sister Stella's clever,
And she doesn't like TV.

----

e Simon can be naughty,
He loves 'Lock and Key'.

----

f Uncle Fred's a farmer,
His beard is short and fair.

----

g Here's our family,
We really love them all.

----

h Grandma Star is quiet,
She wants to paint all day.

Topic worksheet

 Read, write and draw.

1 Picasso's portrait is from 1905. Picasso is a Spanish artist. There are

three children with their .....mother......,  ....

and .... Two of them are wearing ....

.... and one of them has got ....

2 John Singleton Copley's portrait is from 1776. Copley is an American

artist. The portrait is of the artist's family – we can see three

daughters and one son. The boy is wearing a ....

because he's very young.

3 Hulis Mavruk is a Turkish artist but he lives in the United States of

America. In his portrait the .... are both wearing

.... They are walking with their

.... and ....

Reinforcement worksheet 1

- Pupils look at the pictures and write the words on the dashes. They then insert the words into the puzzle to find the missing horizontal word.

Key: 1 balcony, 2 downstairs, 3 upstairs, 4 basement, 5 lift, 6 stairs, 7 city, 8 country.

- *Optional follow-up activity:* Pupils prepare a similar puzzle using the words *flat, town* and *village* and other words from the pictures on page 18 of the Pupil's Book (characters, colours, objects, etc). They then swap and complete the puzzles.

Reinforcement worksheet 2

- Pupils look at the six pictures then write the house numbers and match the two halves of the sentences.

Key: 1 c, 2 e, 3 f, 4 a, 5 d, 6 b.

- *Optional follow-up activity:* In their notebooks, pupils draw a picture of someone in a house. They write one sentence about the person using *needs* or *doesn't need* and one sentence using *can* or *can't*.

Extension worksheet 1

- Pupils solve the riddle to work out the mystery word. They then draw it.

Key: bat cat – b, fat foot – a, lake cake – l, cat mat – c, hot hat – o, bean bear – n, boy box – y.
Balcony.

- *Optional follow-up activity:* Pupils work in groups to prepare a similar puzzle. They then swap puzzles with another group.

Extension worksheet 2

- This can be done as a listening exercise (Track 6) or a reading exercise. Pupils look at the comic strip on page 23 of the Pupil's Book and use the information to solve the crossword.

Key: See Pupil's Book, page 23.

- *Optional follow-up activity:* Pupils think of one more word to add to the crossword and write the clue for their partner to solve.

Song worksheet

- Pupils listen to the song (Track 7) and complete the lyrics.

Key: See Pupil's Book, page 19.

- *Optional follow-up activity:* Pupils work in pairs and play *pelmanism*. They each cut out their verse and picture cards and combine their two packs. Then they place the cards face down on the desk and turn over two cards at a time. If they turn over two matching verse cards, they must read/sing the verse and then put the cards back. If they turn over two matching picture cards, they must name something they can see and then put the cards back. If they turn over the matching verse and picture cards, they keep them.
  The winner is the pupil with the most pairs at the end of the game.

Topic worksheet

- Pupils follow the instructions to draw two houses. They tick the house they think is warmer. They then read the text to check their answer. Pre-teach *warm, insulate, lose, heat* and *saves*.

- *Optional follow-up activity:* Pupils work in groups. They think of ways to save energy in the home. Although their language will be rather limited, you can help them put their ideas into English.

Reinforcement worksheet 1

 Think and write.

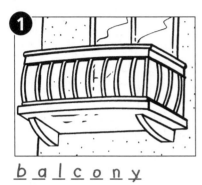

1. <u>b a l c o n y</u>

2. _ _ _ _ _ _ _ _ _

3. _ _ _ _ _ _ _ _

4. _ _ _ _ _ _ _ _

5. _ _ _ _

6. _ _ _ _ _ _ _

7. _ _ _ _

8. The missing word is

_ _ _ _ _ _ _ _

Reinforcement worksheet 2

 Read, look and join.

1 At number 23 <u>twenty-three</u> the girl   **a** doesn't need to use the lift.

2 At number 42 _____ the boy   **b** need to sit down.

3 At number 51 _____ the girl   **c** can go in the lift.

4 At number 74 _____ the woman   **d** needs to drink water.

5 At number 87 _____ the man   **e** can't sit on the sofa.

6 At number 99 _____ the girls   **f** needs to buy some new clothes.

Extension worksheet 1

 Think, write and draw.

My first is in  but not in _b_

.... bat .... cat ....

My second is in  but not in  ....

....

My third is in 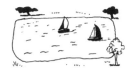 but not in  ....

....

My fourth is in but not in  ....

....

My fifth is in  but not in  ....

....

My sixth is in but not in  ....

....

My seventh is in  but not in ....

....

 What am I? Draw me.

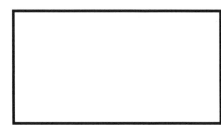

  © Cambridge University Press 2015   Kid's Box Teacher's Resource Book 3

Extension worksheet 2

⏵ **Think and write.**

Across ➡

1 This is the opposite of upstairs.

2 The monster comes upstairs at … .

3 In picture 4, Key says he is not … .

4 This detective's name rhymes with 'sock'.

Down ⬇

5 Mrs Potts thinks her house has got a … .

6 In picture 6, Mrs Potts says her cat is … .

7 This is the noise the monster makes.

8 Lock and Key are sitting on this in picture 1.

Unit 2

Song worksheet

 07 **Listen and do. Sing.**

Home is home ... ,

In a city or a village,

In a house or a ___flat___ .

Home is home!

It's where it's at.

We've got a basement

Under the _____ .

It's got brown stairs

And a purple _____ .

I've got a lift,

It goes up and _____ .

From my balcony,

I can see the _____ .

Upstairs, downstairs,

One floor or _____ .

We live here,

What about _____ ?

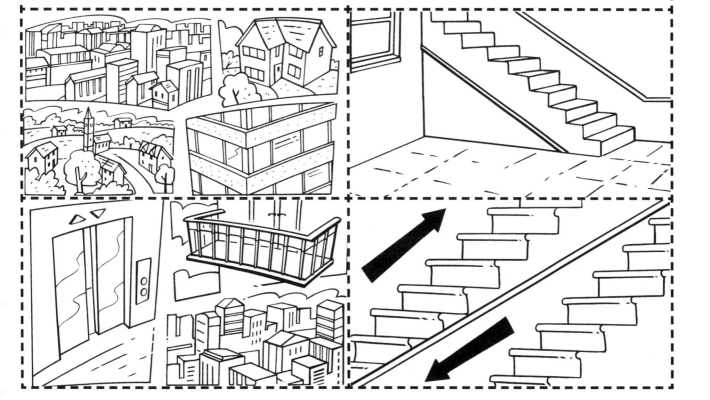

© Cambridge University Press 2015   Kid's Box Teacher's Resource Book 3   **27**

Topic worksheet

 Read, draw and think.

Draw two squares. These are the houses. Draw a triangle on each square. These are the roofs. Draw a rectangle and four squares in each square. These are the doors and the windows. Draw a rectangle on each roof. These are the chimneys. Draw a wall round each house. It is winter. Draw snow on the ground. Draw snow on the roof of house number 1.

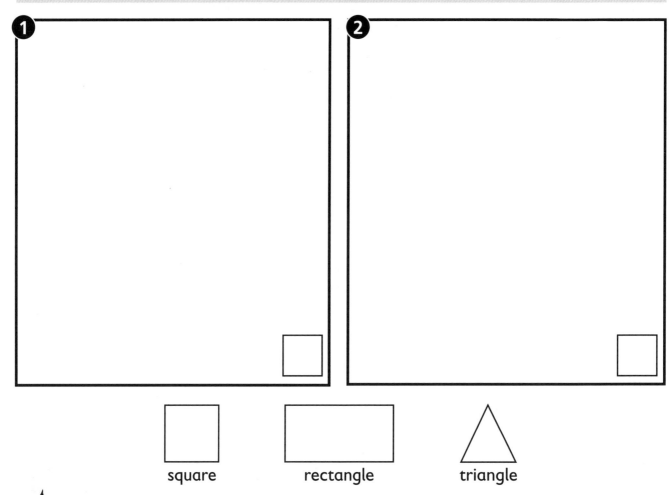

square   rectangle   triangle

 Which is the warm house? Tick (✓) the box.

A good warm house is one that saves energy. A bad cold house is one where all the heat comes out through the roof, walls, doors and windows. It is important to insulate a house so that the house doesn't lose heat. The heat must be inside, not outside. House number 1 is the warm house. Is your answer right?

3 Teacher's notes

Reinforcement worksheet 1

- Pupils read what each character says about his/her daily routine, then look at the pictures and work out who each character is from the time on the clock and the action. They complete the sentences.

Key: 1 It's Peter because Peter gets dressed at eight o'clock. 2 It's Mary because Mary does her homework at five o'clock. 3 It's Jim because Jim wakes up at seven o'clock. 4 It's Jane because Jane has a shower at nine o'clock.

- *Optional follow-up activity:* Pupils work in groups. In their notebooks, pupils draw one of the characters, put a time on the clock and take it in turns to show their pictures to the rest of the group. The winner is the first to work out who the character is.

Reinforcement worksheet 2

- Pupils look at the boy on each day of the week and then use the visual prompts to write sentences using *every day / always, sometimes* and *never.*

Key: 1 He sometimes plays tennis. 2 He sometimes rides a bike. 3 He never rides a horse. 4 He never plays basketball. 5 He sometimes plays the guitar. 6 He always goes swimming. / He goes swimming every day. 7 He sometimes plays a computer game. 8 He always reads a book. / He reads a book every day.

- *Optional follow-up activity:* Pupils draw themselves in their notebooks with all the things they use for their weekly activities. They then write sentences to describe how regularly they do each activity.

Extension worksheet 1

- Pupils use the information in the chart to work out which answer is given by each character.

Key: 1 Paul, Fred, Peter, 2 Peter, Paul, Fred, 3 Peter, Fred, Paul, 4 Fred, Paul, Peter, 5 Fred, Peter/Paul, Peter/Paul.

- *Optional follow-up activity:* Pupils work in pairs. They look at the chart and find two more questions to write for the three characters. They then swap their questions for their partner to answer.

Key: 1 How often do you watch TV?
Paul: Every day. Peter: Every Monday and Friday.
Fred: I never watch TV.
2 How often do you read?
Paul: I never read. Peter: Every Wednesday, Saturday and Sunday. Fred: I never read.

Extension worksheet 2

- This can be done as a listening exercise (Track 8) or a reading exercise. Pupils decide which sentence goes in each gap and then write the numbers in the boxes.

Key: See Pupil's Book, page 33.

- *Optional follow-up activity:* Pupils work in groups of four. Together they decide on four of the story frames and each pupil then cuts out these four frames. They then shuffle all the cards together and deal them out equally. They say *1, 2, 3, pass!* then discard one card face down in front of the player on their left. Each player picks up the new card and decides which card to discard next. The winner is the first player to end up with four cards the same.

Song worksheet

- Pupils listen to the song (Track 9) and fill in the gaps with verbs from the centre. They listen again to check their answers.

Key: See Pupil's Book, page 29.

- *Optional follow-up activity:* Pupils work in pairs. They take it in turns to throw a dice or use the spinner from page 39 (Unit 4 extension worksheet 1). Starting at section 1, they move round the song trail and sing or say the lyrics. For a quicker version, the winner is the first pupil to land on all twelve sections at least once. For a longer version, pupils must land on the sections in order (first, section 1, then section 2).

Topic worksheet

- Ask pupils which animal is as large as three buses to elicit *blue whale.* Ask them to guess whether its heartbeat is fast or slow. Pre-teach words you think pupils may find difficult. Pupils use the words to complete the text.

Key: 1 car, 2 pear, 3 bean, 4 slow, 5 fast

- Pupils look at the pictures and think where each animal might be hiding then read the text to check their answers. Help them to see the connection between hedge and hedgehog.

Key: a 4, b 5, c 6, d 7, e 2, f 1, g 3

- *Optional follow-up activity:* Ask pupils to draw a picture of the countryside and then describe the hiding place they would choose to hibernate in.

Unit 3

Reinforcement worksheet 1

 Read, think and write.

> I wake up at seven o'clock.

> I have a shower at eight o'clock.

Jim

> I wake up at eight o'clock.

> I have a shower at nine o'clock.

Jane

> I have lunch at twelve o'clock.

> I do my homework at four o'clock.

> I have lunch at one o'clock.

> I do my homework at six o'clock.

> I have breakfast at eight o'clock.

> I get dressed at nine o'clock.

> I get dressed at eight o'clock.

> I have breakfast at nine o'clock.

Mary

Peter

> I do my homework at five o'clock.

> I go to bed at eight o'clock.

> I do my homework at three o'clock.

> I go to bed at nine o'clock.

❶ Who is it?

It's Peter because Peter gets dressed at eight o'clock.

❷ Who is it?

....

....

❸ Who is it?

....

....

❹ Who is it?

....

....

Kid's Box Teacher's Resource Book 3   © Cambridge University Press 2015

Unit 3

Reinforcement worksheet 2

 Look and write.

 Monday

 Tuesday

 Wednesday

 Thursday

 Friday

 Saturday

 Sunday

every day   always   sometimes   never

 **1** He sometimes plays tennis.

 5 ....

 **2** ....

 **6** ....

 **3** ....

 **7** ....

 4 ....

 8 ....

© Cambridge University Press 2015   Kid's Box Teacher's Resource Book 3

Unit 3

Extension worksheet 1

★ Read and match.

	Paul	Peter	Fred
Monday	Watch TV	Go to the park Watch TV	Go swimming
Tuesday	Watch TV	Play tennis	Play tennis
Wednesday	Watch TV	Go to the park Read	Go to the park
Thursday	Watch TV	Play football	Play tennis
Friday	Watch TV	Go to the park Watch TV	Go swimming
Saturday	Watch TV	Go swimming Read	Go cycling
Sunday	Watch TV	Read	Play football

1 How often do you play football?

          I never play football.

Fred: Every Sunday.

          Every Thursday.

2 How often do you go to the park?

  ---------- : Every Monday, Wednesday and Friday.

  ---------- : I never go to the park.

  ---------- : I go every Wednesday.

3 How often do you play tennis?

  ---------- : I play every Tuesday.

  ---------- : I play every Tuesday and Thursday.

  ---------- : I never play tennis.

4 How often do you go swimming?

  ---------- : Every Monday and Friday.

  ---------- : I never go swimming.

  ---------- : Every Saturday.

5 How often do you go cycling?

  ---------- : Every Saturday.

  ---------- : I never go cycling.

  ---------- : I never go cycling.

★ Write questions and answers.

--   --

--   --

--   --

--   --

   Kid's Box Teacher's Resource Book 3   © Cambridge University Press 2015   **PHOTOCOPIABLE**

Extension worksheet 2

08▶ Think and write.

Know(s)

Everybody knows detectives are very clever.

[ ]

We all know detectives work a lot and get up before you and me.

[1]

Sometimes / never

we never get up before ten o'clock.

[ ]

We're very quiet so they never know we're behind them.

[ ]

Yes, sometimes we follow people.

[ ]

Questions

what do you think?

[ ]

Are they quiet?

[ ]

Where are you?

[ ]

And are they very clever?

[ ]

Do these detectives work a lot?

[ ]

 Kid's Box Teacher's Resource Book 3

Unit 3 Song worksheet

09 **Listen and write. Sing.**

1 I ___wake up___ in the morning,

I .... and I .... to bed.
Oooh yes, Oooh yes, Oooh yes,
every day, every day.

2 I ....
for breakfast,

Before I ....
my dinner.

11

10

I .... my
hands

3 I ....
.... and I
....
Oooh yes, every
day.

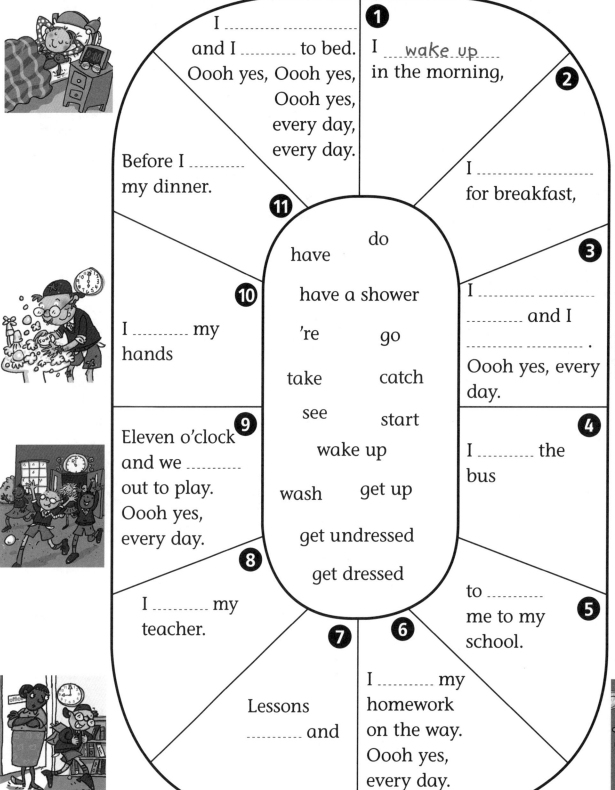

do
have
have a shower
're   go
take   catch
see   start
wake up
wash   get up
get undressed
get dressed

9 Eleven o'clock
and we ....
out to play.
Oooh yes,
every day.

4 I .... the
bus

8

I .... my
teacher.

7

Lessons
.... and

6

I .... my
homework
on the way.
Oooh yes,
every day.

to ....
me to my
school.

5

Unit 3 Topic worksheet

 Use the words to complete the text.

| quick | pear | car | slow | bean |

The heart of a blue whale is the size of a **1** .... Its heartbeat is 20 beats per minute. Your heart is the size of a **2** .... Your heartbeat is about 90 beats per minute. The heart of a mouse is the size of a **3** .... A mouse heartbeat is 500 beats per minute. Big animals have **4** .... heartbeats and little animals have **5** .... heartbeats.

 Match the animals with their hiding places.

Look at the picture of the countryside. You can't see the animals because they are hibernating. Hibernation is a long sleep in the winter. When an animal is sleeping, its heartbeat is very slow.

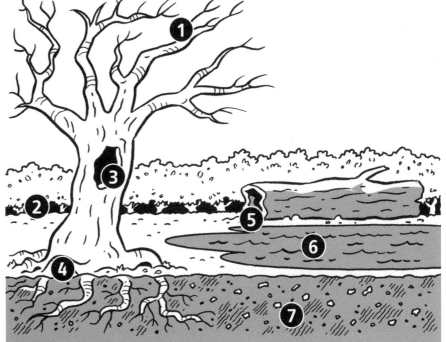

 Now read and check.

Mice sleep in a ball under trees. They sleep for seven months! Hedgehogs sleep under hedges. Frogs sleep under the water in ponds. Squirrels sleep at the top of trees. Worms sleep under the ground. Snakes sleep under logs on the ground. Bees sleep in holes in trees.

© Cambridge University Press 2015 Kid's Box Teacher's Resource Book 3

Teacher's notes

Reinforcement worksheet 1

- Pupils look at the pictures and write the names of the corresponding buildings below. They then find the words in the wordsearch.

Key: 1 market, 2 sports centre, 3 library, 4 swimming pool, 5 bank, 6 supermarket, 7 bus station, 8 cinema.

- *Optional follow-up activity:* Pupils copy the remaining letters in the wordsearch (in order from left to right and top to bottom) to find (1) a task to do and (2) the name of what the children are looking at on page 36 of the Pupil's Book.

Key: (1) Draw a sign for a shop. Ask your friends to think of the shop. How many shops and signs are the same? (2) map.

Reinforcement worksheet 2

- Pupils follow the instructions to make their way round the grid. They name where they are and select the most appropriate *must* sentence.

Key: 1 At the library. We must be quiet. 2 At the bus station. We must buy a bus ticket. 3 At the market. We must pay for the fish and fruit. 4 At the supermarket. We must pay for the milk and biscuits. 5 At the swimming pool. We must take a towel. 6 At the cinema. We must sit down.

- *Optional follow-up activity:* Pupils decide on a new route and tell their partners how to move round the town.

Extension worksheet 1

- Pupils start at the bus station. It is easier to give each pupil a dice, but if you haven't got enough, ask them to cut out the spinner, mount it on card and push a pencil through the centre. Pupils spin the spinner and move that number of spaces. They tick the box next to the action they can do there and complete the sentence with the name of the place. They continue moving round the board from one square to the next, moving in any direction until they have done all the errands.

Key: shoe shop, café, library, clothes shop, bus station, sports centre, park, hospital, swimming pool, supermarket, toy shop, market.

- *Optional follow-up activity:* Pupils play in pairs or small groups. The winner is the first to complete the errands.

Extension worksheet 2

- This can be done as a listening exercise (Track 10) or a reading exercise. Pupils look at the negative sentences and phrases at the bottom of the page and make them affirmative. They then decide which frame each affirmative sentence belongs to.

Key: See Pupil's Book, page 41.

- *Optional follow-up activity:* Pupils work in groups of four. Each pupil cuts out the six frames. They then shuffle all the cards together and deal them out equally. Working in a clockwise direction, pupils take it in turns to place a card on the table. The card must be frame one or the next frame in a line (frame two goes after frame one, frame three after frame two, etc). If a pupil cannot place a card, he/she must pass. The winner is the first player to get rid of all his/her cards.

Song worksheet

- Pupils listen to the song (Track 11) and complete the lyrics. They cut out the six pages and staple them together to make a book. They then cut along the dotted line. As pupils turn the pages, they will read mostly silly questions and some sensible ones.

Key: See Pupil's Book, page 39.

- *Optional follow-up activity:* Pupils work in groups. One pupil turns the pages of his/her book, without the others looking, and chooses a combination which he/she then reads out loud. The first pupil to turn their pages to that sentence has the next go.

Topic worksheet

- Pupils make a mini book. First they fold along fold 1, then they cut along the dotted lines. Next they fold along fold 2 and the remaining two lines. When all the folds have been made, pupils open the sheet up and fold along fold 2 again. They join point a to point b, point c to point d and, finally, point e to point f. Once they have made the book, they decide on one item from each page and subtract from the initial sum the price of the item they have chosen so that by the end of the book, they have money left over from their shopping trip.

- *Optional follow-up activity:* Pupils take it in turns to read their shopping stories. How many of them have ended up with the same sum?

Reinforcement worksheet 1

 Think and write. Find the words.

1 market   **2** _____   **3** _____   **4** _____

5 _____   **6** _____   **7** _____   **8** _____

s	p	o	r	t	s	c	e	n	t	r	e
u	w	c	d	r	a	w	a	s	b	i	g
p	n	i	f	o	r	a	s	h	u	o	p
e	.	n	m	a	r	k	e	t	s	a	s
r	k	e	y	m	l	o	u	r	s	f	r
m	i	m	e	n	i	d	s	t	t	o	t
a	h	a	i	n	b	n	k	o	a	f	t
r	h	e	s	h	r	o	g	p	t	.	h
k	o	w	m	b	a	n	k	p	i	a	n
e	y	s	h	o	r	p	s	a	o	n	d
t	s	i	g	n	y	s	a	r	n	o	e
t	h	e	s	a	m	e	?	m	a	p	l

Reinforcement worksheet 2

 Look, follow and write.

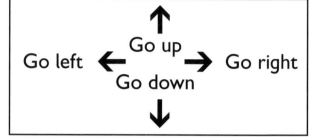

Go up
Go left ← → Go right
Go down

~~We must be quiet.~~

We must pay for the milk and biscuits.

We must pay for the fish and fruit.

We must sit down.

We must take a towel.

We must buy a bus ticket.

START

1 Go up two, go right one. Where are you? At the library. We must be quiet.

2 Go up one, go left one. Where are you? _____

3 Go up one, go right two. Where are you? _____

4 Go down one, go right two. Where are you? _____

5 Go down two, go left one. Where are you? _____

6 Go down one, go left one. Where are you? _____

Unit 4
Extension worksheet 1

Think and write.

☐ Catch a bus at the _bus station_.

☐ Have a drink at the _____ .

☐ Take some books back at /

to the _____ .

☐ Buy some shoes at the _____ .

☐ Buy a coat at the _____ .

☐ Play tennis at the _____ .

☐ Fly a kite at / in the _____ .

☐ See the doctor at the _____ .

☐ Go swimming at the _____ .

☐ Buy some biscuits at the _____ .

☐ Buy some skates at the _____ .

☐ Buy some fruit at the _____ .

Extension worksheet 2

 10 Change and write.

The comic strip:

Lock and Key are looking for work on the computer.

Hmm, Lottie Cash, the bank robber. **a** _____

No problem, Lock!

I need some money. **b** _____

Today is a lovely day for shopping in the city.

Come on then, let's go. **c** _____

d _____ It's Lottie Cash, the bank robber! She's going to the bank now.

We must stop her! We need to get there before her.

e _____ , Lottie Cash!

Lottie who?

Don't touch her money!

What? Not you again, Mr Key!

Stand up, Key. **f** _____

No problem, Lock!

1 I don't love shopping. → I love shopping. [c]

2 You and I don't need to talk! → _____ [ ]

3 We can't find her. → _____ [ ]

4 Don't give me that money → _____ [ ]

5 I mustn't go to the bank. → _____ [ ]

6 It isn't her! → _____ [ ]

Song worksheet

 Listen and do. Sing.

Must I make	Must I wear
my bed _____ , Dad?	_____ , Dad?
Yes, you must.	Yes, you must.
Must I go to	Must I do
_____ , Dad?	_____ , Dad?
Yes, you must.	Yes, you must.
Must I clean	Can I play in
_____ , Dad?	_____ , Dad?
Yes, you must.	Yes, you can!

Unit 4 Topic worksheet

Make and write.

b •

fold 2

In the furniture shop

I want _____

The price is _____

Now I have

£ _____

I _____

e •

75p

90p

60p

70p

£5.20

£6.55

£4.65

£3.70   **f** •

In the fruit shop

I want _____

The price is _____

Now I have

£ _____

I _____

a •

fold 1

£ _____

Now I have _____

d •

£1.95

£2.35

£1.80

£2.05

In the toy shop

I want _____

The price is _____

Now I have

£10.00

I _____

I'm going shopping.
I have £10.00.

c •

42

Kid's Box Teacher's Resource Book 3   © Cambridge University Press 2015

PHOTOCOPIABLE

Reinforcement worksheet 1

- Pupils follow the letter trail in the word maze from *In* to *Out*. They write the words in the patients' answers. They then copy each of the remaining letters (in order from left to right and top to bottom) onto the dashes to find the doctor's question.

Key: What's the matter? 1 temperature, 2 headache, 3 toothache, 4 stomach-ache, 5 earache, 6 backache.

- *Optional follow-up activity:* Pupils draw an empty grid in their notebooks to prepare a similar puzzle for a friend, using the words 'cough' and 'cold' and two words from the trail above.

Reinforcement worksheet 2

- Pupils cut out the two spinners, mount them on card and push pencils through the centres. They spin spinner one to write the *don't* sentence and spinner two to write the *mustn't* sentence. They then tick the sentences if the combination makes sense and cross them if they don't.

- *Optional follow-up activity:* Pupils work in pairs, A and B. They take it in turns to spin the *mustn't* spinner, then they both spin the *don't* spinner. They get a point if the two sentences go together. The winner is the player with the most points.

Extension worksheet 1

- Pupils use the information from the chart to complete the dialogues.

- *Optional follow-up activity:* Pupils work in pairs, A and B. Each pupil thinks up a new combination of ailments. Pupil A is the doctor and B the patient, and then they swap roles.

Extension worksheet 2

- This can be done as a listening exercise (Track 12) or a reading exercise. Pupils look at the comic strip on page 51 of the Pupil's Book and use the information to solve the crossword.

Key: See Pupil's Book, page 51.

- *Optional follow-up activity:* Pupils think of one more word to add to the crossword and write the clue for their partner to solve.

Song worksheet

- Pupils listen to the song (Track 13) twice and decide which group of song lines goes where. The first time they listen, they write the letter and the second time they check their answers. They then copy the lyrics onto the lines in the correct order.

Key: See Pupil's Book, page 53.

- *Optional follow-up activity:* Pupils work in groups. They take it in turns to sing/say one of the pairs of lines. The first person to sing/say the following pair has the next go.

Topic worksheet

- Pupils count how many times in a minute they can do the actions. They write their answers in the chart.

- *Optional follow-up activity:* Pupils mingle asking *How many times in a minute can you … ?* They write the answers in the chart and compare scores.

Unit 5

Reinforcement worksheet 1

Look, follow and write.

In ➡

t	w	h	t	o	a	t	a	r	a
e	'	s	e	o			e		c
m	p	c	h	t	h		e	e	h
	e	a		a		h	b		
a	r	d	t	h	c	a	c	a	c
t	e	a	h	e	e	-			k
u	h		s	t	h		c	a	
r	e	m	a		o	c		h	e
		t	t	m	a	e	r	?	

➡ Out

_____ ___ _____

1 I've got a __temperature__ .

2 I've got a
-------------------------- .

3 I've got a
-------------------------- .

4 I've got a
-------------------------- .

5 I've got an
-------------------------- .

6 I've got a
-------------------------- .

Kid's Box Teacher's Resource Book 3   © Cambridge University Press 2015   **PHOTOCOPIABLE**

Reinforcement worksheet 2

★ Play and write.

1 We mustn't run. – Don't run. ✓

2 We mustn't get up. – Don't sing. ✗

3 _____ ☐

4 _____ ☐

5 _____ ☐

6 _____ ☐

7 _____ ☐

8 _____ ☐

9 _____ ☐

10 _____ ☐

1

Don't talk in the library.

Don't go out.

Don't sing.

Don't eat sweets.

Don't run.

Don't get up.

2

We mustn't talk in the library.

We mustn't go out.

We mustn't sing.

We mustn't eat sweets.

We mustn't run.

We mustn't get up.

© Cambridge University Press 2015   Kid's Box Teacher's Resource Book 3

Extension worksheet 1

 Read, think and write.

	cough	cold	temperature	earache	stomach-ache	headache
Fred		✓	✓	✓		✓
Sue	✓	✓				✓
Alex			✓		✓	✓
Lucy	✓	✓	✓	✓		

Example

Doctor: Hello. What's the matter?
Fred: I've got a cold and a headache.
Doctor: Have you got a temperature?
Fred: Yes, and I've got an earache.
Doctor: Take this with every meal.
Fred: Thank you. Goodbye.
Doctor: Goodbye.

Doctor: Hello. What's the matter?
Sue: I've got a __cough__ and a
_____ .
Doctor: Have you got a _____ ?
Sue: No, but I've got a _____ .
Doctor: Take this with every meal.
Sue: Thank you. Goodbye.
Doctor: Goodbye.

Doctor: Hello. _____
_____ ?
Alex: I've got a _____ .
Doctor: Have you got a _____ ?
Alex: Yes, and I've got a _____ .
Doctor: _____ this with every
_____ .
Alex: Thank you. _____ .
Doctor: Goodbye.

Doctor: _____
_____
Lucy: _____
_____
Doctor: _____
Lucy: _____
_____
Doctor: _____
_____
Lucy: _____
Doctor: _____

Kid's Box Teacher's Resource Book 3   © Cambridge University Press 2015   **PHOTOCOPIABLE**

Unit 5 — Extension worksheet 2

⑫ Think and write.

2	t o o

Across →

1 In picture 2, Miss Rich says, 'This is my _____ painting.'

2 This word in picture 6 rhymes with 'blue'.

3 What's the matter with Key in picture 6? He's got a _____ - _____ .

Down ↓

4 In picture 4, Key says, 'I can't _____.'

5 In picture 5, how many cakes are on the plate?

6 This cake is made from a vegetable.

7 Miss Rich has a painting called 'The _____'.

8 Which cake does Lock take in picture 4?

Song worksheet

 (13) Listen and do. Sing.

a Dance, dance, dance.
Hop, skip and jump.
Come on you know it's fun.

b Move, move, move.
To be fit and well.
Come on move your body …

c Dance, dance, dance.
Don't stop until you drop.
Come on you know it's fun.

d Move, move, move.
Move your body.

e Let's have a good time.
Run, swim and climb.

f Move, move, move.
Move your body.

g Move, move, move.
To be fit and well.
Come on move your body …

h Move, move, move.
Move your body.

i Let's have a good time.
Run, swim and climb.

b   Move, move, move.
    To be fit and well.
    Come on move your body.

Unit 5 Topic worksheet

 Do and write.

There are 60 seconds in one minute.

How many times in a minute can you …

| stand up and sit down? | jump? | hop? | write 'Hello'? |

Name	Stand up and sit down	Jump	Hop	Write 'Hello'

© Cambridge University Press 2015   Kid's Box Teacher's Resource Book 3

Reinforcement worksheet 1

- Pupils look at the pictures and read the clues to complete the crossword.

Key: Across: 1 leaf, 2 river, 3 plant.
Down: 3 picnic, 4 lake, 5 grass, 6 forest, 7 field.

- *Optional follow-up activity:* Pupils think of one more word to add to the crossword and write the clue for their partner to solve.

Reinforcement worksheet 2

- Pupils use a dice or the spinner from page 39 to move up and down the statements and questions for the punctuation marks. With the first throw/spin, they land on an exclamation and with the second, a suggestion. They then write the sentences on the lines below. If the two make sense together, they write *Yes, please.* and if not, *No, thank you.*

- *Optional follow-up activity:* Pupils work in groups of four. One pupil makes a statement about a problem. The first pupil to offer a sensible suggestion has the next go.

Extension worksheet 1

- Pupils look at the picture and label the places *forest, river, lake* or *field.* They then read the text and transfer the information to the chart (by putting ticks and crosses). They then work out the name of each of the characters.

Key: painting – Peter, with sheep – Vicky, fishing from boat – Jill, in forest with dog – Mary, fishing in river – Bill.

- *Optional follow-up activity:* Pupils work in groups of four. One pupil describes the likes and dislikes of one of the characters (changing the order of activities in the chart, for example, *She likes painting. She doesn't like water. She likes animals but she doesn't like fishing.*). The first pupil to guess which character it is has the next go.

Extension worksheet 2

- This can be done as a listening exercise (Track 14) or a reading exercise. Pupils decide which sentence goes in each gap and then write the numbers in the boxes.

Key: See Pupil's Book, page 59.

- *Optional follow-up activity:* Pupils work in groups of four. Together they decide on four of the story frames and each pupil then cuts out these four frames. They then shuffle all the cards together and deal them out equally. They say *1, 2, 3, pass!* then discard one card face down in front of the player on their left. Each player picks up the new card and decides which card to discard next. The winner is the first player to end up with four cards the same.

Song worksheet

- Pupils listen to the song (Track 15) and identify the pictograms. They then write each missing word on the dotted line.

Key: See Pupil's Book, page 57.

- *Optional follow-up activity:* Pupils write a short text about themselves using five pictograms. Pupils work in pairs, A and B. They swap texts. Pupil A reads Pupil B's text and vice versa. To do so, they will need to interpret the pictograms.

Topic worksheet

- Pre-teach words you think the pupils may find difficult. Pupils write the parts of the plant. Next they read the sentences and match them with the pictures.

- They copy their favourite fact.

Key: leaves, fruit, roots, seeds

Key: 1 b, 2 i, 3 f, 4 c, 5 g, 6 h, 7 d, 8 j, 9 e, 10 a

- *Optional follow-up activity:* Help your pupils understand the dimensions by asking them, for example, to stand in a circle with a diameter of three metres or mark the length of the leaves, roots and trees on the playground floor. Time how long it takes them to walk, jump, run, etc the same length.

Reinforcement worksheet 1

★ **Think and write.**

Across →
1. This is green.
   It grows on a tree.
2. Fish swim here.
3. This has leaves.

Down ↓
3. You eat this outside.
4. This word rhymes with 'cake'.
5. This is green and grows on the ground.
6. There are lots of trees here.
7. Horses sometimes live here.

Reinforcement worksheet 2

 Play and write.

!	?
1 My bag's big!	**1** Shall we have a drink?
2 I'm tired!	**2** Shall I open the window?
3 I'm thirsty!	**3** Shall I close the window?
4 I'm hungry!	**4** Shall we sit down?
5 I'm cold!	**5** Shall I make lunch?
6 I'm hot!	**6** Shall I carry it for you?

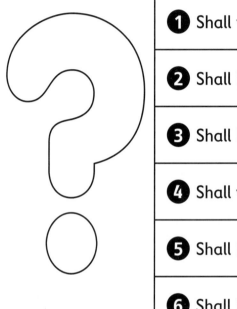

Examples

I'm cold!   Shall we sit down?   No, thank you.

My bag's big!   Shall I carry it for you?   Yes, please.

1 ....

2 ....

3 ....

4 ....

5 ....

6 ....

Kid's Box Teacher's Resource Book 3   © Cambridge University Press 2015   **PHOTOCOPIABLE**

Extension worksheet 1

Read, think and write. Complete the table.

Vicky

Five friends are in the countryside. Their names are Peter, Vicky, Mary, Jill and Bill. Vicky and Bill can't paint, but Mary, Jill and Peter are good at painting. Mary, Vicky and Peter don't like fishing, but Bill and Jill love fishing. Jill fishes from her boat. Peter, Vicky and Mary don't like the water. Vicky, Mary and Bill love animals and Mary has got a dog.

	Water	Animals	Painting	Fishing
Peter				
Vicky			✗	
Mary				
Jill				
Bill				

Extension worksheet 2

 ⁴ Think and write.

1 ____ — Great idea, Lock.

2 ____ — Yes, Key. 3 ____

TECS 2

4 ____ 5 ____ — No thank you, Mr Key. 6 ____

Are you hungry, Lock? 7 ____

8 ____ We've got a big picnic.

Are you cold, Mrs Potts? 9 ____ — No, thank you. It's hot. I don't need a blanket.

Yes, Key! — Good idea!

Well, 10 ____ No problem, 11 ____

Do it!

Don't be silly, Key. ☐

Go and stand in front of our car. ☐

Please go and ask her. ☐

Let's go to the countryside for a picnic, Key. ☐ 1

Shall I/we?

Shall I take a photo of you, Mrs Potts? ☐

Shall I go to the river and catch some fish to eat? ☐

Shall we ask Mrs Potts, too? ☐

Shall I put this blanket on you? ☐

can/can't

I can go for a long walk up the mountain. ☐

I can take one of the lake. ☐

I can't get you food or a blanket and I can't help you ... ☐

54   Kid's Box Teacher's Resource Book 3   © Cambridge University Press 2015   **PHOTOCOPIABLE**

Song worksheet

 Listen and do. Sing.

People, people here or there.

People, people everywhere.

Different colours, different skin

Bodies that are [image] fat............, bodies that are [image] ....

Some are [image] .... , some are [image] ....

With [image] ....that's short or [image] .... that's long

Straight, curly, dark or fair

Different [image] .... , different [image] ....

People, different people, different,

Hungry, thirsty, [image] .... or [image] .... ,

[image] .... or [image] .... , good or bad

People are [image] .... , people are small

People are short, people are [image] ....

People, different people, different,

Funny, naughty, [image] .... or tired

Clever, beautiful, loud or quiet

People, people here or there.

People, people everywhere.

© Cambridge University Press 2015   Kid's Box Teacher's Resource Book 3

Unit 6 Topic worksheet

★ **Complete the parts of the plant.**

l _ _ _ _ _   f _ _ _ _   r _ _ _ _   s _ _ _ _

★ **Read and match.**

1. The seed of the Coco de Mer is the size of a football.

2. Bamboo can grow nearly one metre a day.

3. The leaves of the giant water lily have a diameter of 3 metres.

4. The flower of the Rafflesia is the size of the wheel of a tractor. The flower smells very bad.

5. A strawberry has more than 100 seeds. It is the only fruit with seeds on the outside.

6. The dwarf willow tree is the size of a pencil.

7. Some sequoia trees in California, USA, are the size of the Statue of Liberty.

8. The Venus flytrap is a carnivorous plant. It needs 10 days to eat a fly.

9. The leaves of the Raffia palm can be 25 metres long.

10. The roots of some plants in very hot countries grow to 60 metres to find water.

★ **Copy your favourite fact.**

Reinforcement worksheet 1

- Pupils use the international flag code to decipher the names of the animals. They then draw them.

Key: 1 lion, 2 shark, 3 bear, 4 whale, 5 dolphin, 6 panda, 7 bat, 8 parrot, 9 kangaroo.

- *Optional follow-up activity:* Pupils work in pairs. They use the code to write the name of another animal. They then swap words, decode them and draw the animal.

Reinforcement worksheet 2

- Pupils look at the animal pictures and answer the questions in the first grid. They put the answers in the same position on the second grid and then work out the missing numbers by getting each horizontal, vertical and diagonal line to add up to 18. They look at the pictures to complete the sentences at the bottom of the page.

Key: Top line: 3, 10, 5. Middle line: 8, 6, 4. Bottom line: 7, 2, 9.

- *Optional follow-up activity:* In their notebooks, pupils draw a grid and write the questions missing from grid one.

Extension worksheet 1

- Pupils look at the pictures and the adjective below each one. They use the information to write comparative sentences. They then affix a photo of their family, or draw it, and write comparative sentences about the family members.

Key: 1 John is cleaner than Peter. 2 Mary is thinner than Vicky. 3 Fred is longer than Jack. 4 Sue is happier than Bill. 5 Paul is stronger than Jim. 6 Lucy is smaller than Daisy.

- *Optional follow-up activity:* Pupils work in groups and play *Chinese whispers*. They stand in a line or sit in a circle. One child whispers one of his/her comparative sentences to the child next to him/her. He/she then whispers it to the next person, etc. The last child in the group says the sentence aloud. This sentence is compared with the original and pupils give each other a high five if they've got it right. They can then reorganize the group to play again. If you wish to make the game competitive, two teams can play against each other.

Extension worksheet 2

- This can be done as a listening exercise (Track 16) or a reading exercise. Pupils look at the negative sentences at the bottom of the page and make them affirmative. They then decide which frame each sentence belongs to.

Key: See Pupil's Book, page 69.

- *Optional follow-up activity:* Pupils work in groups of four. Each pupil cuts out the six frames. They then shuffle all the cards together and deal them out equally. Working in a clockwise direction, they take it in turns to place a card on the table. The card must be frame one or the next frame in a line (frame two goes after frame one, frame three after frame two and so on). If a pupil cannot place a card, he/she must pass. The winner is the first player to get rid of all his/her cards.

Song worksheet

- Pupils listen to the song (Track 17). For squares 1–5, they copy the final line of each verse onto the dotted line. For squares 6–10, they draw the animals in the space provided.

Key: See Pupil's Book, page 67.

- *Optional follow-up activity:* Pupils work in groups and play *Slam!* They cut out the cards. One pupil (the caller) puts his/her cards in a pile face down, whilst the rest place their cards face up on the table in front of them. The caller turns over the first card from his/her pile, making sure the others can't see it, and reads the lyrics. The other pupils listen and slam their hand down on the correct card. The first child to slam wins two points. In the case of a draw, pupils get one point each. Play continues until the caller has read (or sung!) all of his/her song cards. The winner of the game is the pupil with the most points. He/she becomes the caller in the next round. If you wish for a quieter game, pupils can pick up rather than slam the correct card.

Topic worksheet

- Pre-teach *omnivore, carnivore, herbivore, pig.* Pupils read the text then work out the anagrams to put the names of the animals in the corresponding columns depending on whether they are herbivores, carnivores or omnivores.

Key: Herbivores: sheep, cow, elephant, rabbit; Carnivores: dolphin, crocodile, lion, frog; Omnivores: pig, mouse, monkey, bear.

- *Optional follow-up activity:* Pupils work in pairs. They cut out the individual animal cards and shuffle them, each keeping their own pack. On the word *Go!* they each turn over their top card. If they are the same, the first pupil to say *Snap!* wins the cards (plus any others that haven't been won). If the cards are different, they each turn over the next card and play continues. The winner is the pupil who has the most cards at the end of the game.

Reinforcement worksheet 1

⭐ **Find, write and draw.**

a b c d e f g h

1. Lion

2. _ _ _ _ _ _

3. _ _ _ _

4. _ _ _ _ _ _

5. _ _ _ _ _ _ _ _

6. _ _ _ _ _ _

7. _ _ _

8. _ _ _ _ _ _ _

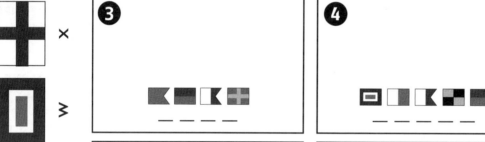
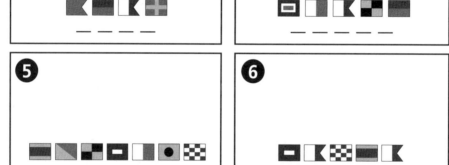
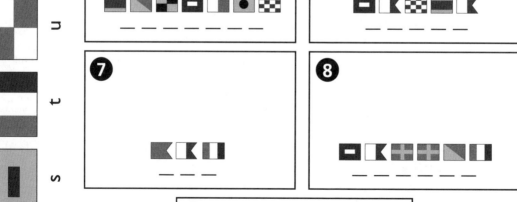

9. _ _ _ _ _ _ _ _ _ _

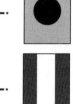

Kid's Box Teacher's Resource Book 3   © Cambridge University Press 2015

Reinforcement worksheet 2

⭐ **Look and write.**

❶ What number is the cleaner panda?		What number is the bigger kangaroo?
	What number is the dirtier parrot?	
What number is the thinner dolphin?		What number is the weaker lion?

❷ 3		

The dirtier panda is picture 8 ....

The smaller kangaroo ....

The cleaner parrot ....

The fatter dolphin ....

The stronger lion ....

Extension worksheet 1

 Look and write.

John	Peter	Mary	Vicky		Fred

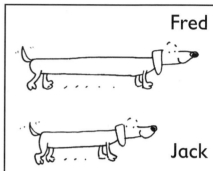

clean   thin   long

1 John is cleaner than Peter.

2 _____

3 _____

Sue	Bill	Paul	Jim	Daisy	Lucy

happy   strong   small

4 _____
_____

5 _____

6 _____

Example

I'm taller than my brother.

I'm _____ than _____ .

_____

_____

_____

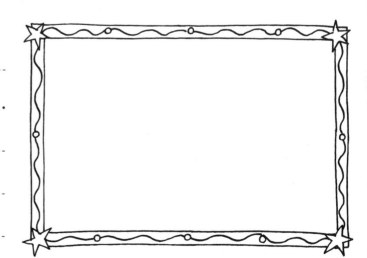

Kid's Box Teacher's Resource Book 3   © Cambridge University Press 2015   **PHOTOCOPIABLE**

Extension worksheet 2

 🔵 **Change and write.**

a _____ Lock and Key are in their office. It's hot. They're tired and thirsty.

Hmm... Robin Motors, the car thief.

Yes, let's go to that new café in town.

b _____ Shall we stop?

Don't look, Key, but **c** _____ next to us.

No, that man's uglier than Robin Motors. His nose is bigger and his hair's longer.

Sssh. Be quiet, Key. **d** _____ , and he's looking at us.

That's not him, Lock. He's the wrong man. **e** _____ and taller than him.

Sssh, Key! Everybody can hear you!

But he isn't Robin Motors!

Oh yes he is, and ... **f** _____

1 He isn't taking our car! → He's taking our car! | f |

2 He can't hear you → | |

3 It isn't Thursday morning. → | |

4 Robin Motors isn't sitting at the table → | |

5 I don't need a cold drink. → | |

6 Robin Motors isn't thinner → | |

17 **Listen and do. Sing.**

1 I'm walking,
I'm walking.
What can I see?
I can see a lion and
it's bigger than me.

6

I can see a bat and it's smaller than me.

2 I'm swimming,
I'm swimming.
What can I see?

7

I can see a lion and it's bigger than me.

3 I'm standing,
I'm standing.
What can I see?

8

I can see a snake and it's thinner than me.

4 I'm hiding,
I'm hiding.
What can I see?

9

I can see a monkey and it's naughtier than me.

5 I'm sitting,
I'm sitting.
What can I see?

10

I can see a shark and it's uglier than me.

Kid's Box Teacher's Resource Book 3   © Cambridge University Press 2015   **PHOTOCOPIABLE**

Topic worksheet

 Read, match and write.

All animals need to eat. Some animals eat plants and fruit. They are called herbivores. Other animals eat meat from animals. They are called carnivores. Some animals eat plants and animals. They are called omnivores.

Herbivores	Carnivores	Omnivores
sheep	----------	----------
----------	----------	----------
----------	----------	----------
----------	----------	----------

sephe   arbe

woc

ouems

nkmyeo

lehepatn

rtaibb

gip   nolhdpi

nilo

grfo

rcocoilde

Teacher's notes

Reinforcement worksheet 1

- Pupils look at the pictures and use the information to complete the sentences. They then affix a photo or draw themselves on holiday somewhere and complete the text about themselves.

Key: 1 sunny, T-shirt, shorts, hat, ice cream, 2 mountains, cold, snowing, coat, scarf, boots, bear, 3 countryside, wet, sunny, jacket, trousers, boots, rainbow.

- *Optional follow-up activity:* Pupils cut out the text they have written and place their personal pictures on the table. They take it in turns to read their text and the rest have to work out which photo/picture is being described. The bigger the group, the more challenging this is.

Reinforcement worksheet 2

- Pupils use the information in the calendar to complete the sentences about where the characters were on each day of the week. They then look at the picture, find what day of the week it is (Friday) and look for the three characters to see who is lying. Explain *telling the truth*.

Key: Peter isn't telling the truth.

- *Optional follow-up activity:* Pupils choose a different day of the week and draw two of the characters doing what they said they were doing and the third doing something different. They swap pictures to work out who isn't telling the truth. To make this easier, pupils can decide on a colour for each character and draw stick figures.

Extension worksheet 1

- Pupils cut out the two spinners, mount them on card and push pencils through the centres. They spin spinner one to write the weather sentence and spinner two to write the clothes sentence. They will have to decide between *was* and *were*. They then put an exclamation mark (!) if the combination doesn't make sense and a tick (✓) if it does.

- *Optional follow-up activity:* Pupils work in pairs, A and B. They take it in turns to spin the weather spinner then they both spin the clothes spinner. They get a point if the sentences from the two spinners go together. The winner is the player with the most points.

Extension worksheet 2

- This can be done as a listening exercise (Track 18) or a reading exercise. Pupils look at the comic strip on page 77 of the Pupil's Book and use the information to solve the crossword.

Key: See Pupil's Book, page 77.

- *Optional follow-up activity:* Pupils think of one more word to add to the crossword and write the clue for their partner to solve.

Song worksheet

- Pupils listen to the song (Track 19) and replace the rhyming words in capital letters with the correct words. They then write the rhyming pairs in the table.

Key: See Pupil's Book, page 75.

- *Optional follow-up activity:* In their notebooks, pupils write as many more rhyming words as they can.

Topic worksheet

- Pre-teach words you think the pupils may find difficult. Pupils read the text and answer the questions. They colour in the frame of the harp and then sew over the strings. (NB. Photocopy this worksheet onto card. You will also need to provide needles, thread and scissors.) To begin with, pupils should mark all the holes with a needle and then push the thread through from the back so that the loose ends are not seen.

- *Optional follow-up activity:* Pupils discover which other regions have Celtic music. If possible, play a piece of Celtic music for pupils to listen to. Ask them what instruments they can hear.

Reinforcement worksheet 1

⭐ **Look, think and write.**

❶ This is me on holiday by the sea. It's hot and s u n n y. I'm wearing a T- s h i r t, s _ _ _ _ _ and a h _ _ . I'm eating an i_ _ _ _ _ _ _ .

❷ This is me on holiday in the m_ _ _ _ _ _ _ _ . It's c _ _ _ and it's s_ _ _ _ _ _ . I'm wearing a c _ _ _ , a s_ _ _ _ and b_ _ _ _ . I can see a b _ _ _ .

❸ This is me on holiday in the c_ _ _ _ _ _ _ _ _ _ . It's w _ _ and s_ _ _ _ . I'm wearing a j_ _ _ _ _ , t_ _ _ _ _ _ _ and b_ _ _ _ . I can see a r_ _ _ _ _ _ .

This is me on holiday _____
_____ .

It's _____ .

I'm wearing _____ .

I _____ .

© Cambridge University Press 2015   Kid's Box Teacher's Resource Book 3

Reinforcement worksheet 2

Think, write and look.

	Monday 11th	Tuesday 12th	Wednesday 13th	Thursday 14th	Friday 15th
Peter 	at the hospital (all day)	at school (all day)	in the countryside (all day)	at the café (at lunchtime)	at the sports centre (7 o'clock)
Jane and Tom	at the supermarket (in the morning)	in the park (at lunchtime)	at the farm (all day)	at the beach (all afternoon)	at the sports centre (7 o'clock)

Vicky: Where were you?

Peter: On Monday, I was at the hospital all day.

On Tuesday, I was at school all day.

On Wednesday, I was ——————————————— .

On Thursday, ——————————————— .

On Friday, ——————————————— .

Jane and Tom: On Monday, we were ——————————————— .

On Tuesday, we were ——————————————— .

On Wednesday, ——————————————— .

On Thursday, ——————————————— .

On Friday, ——————————————— .

Who isn't telling the truth? ———————————————————————

Kid's Box Teacher's Resource Book 3   © Cambridge University Press 2015   **PHOTOCOPIABLE**

Unit 8

Extension worksheet 1

 Play and write.

On Monday, it was ...hot... . My ...coat.. was / ~~were~~ blue. `!`

On Tuesday, it was ...snowing... . My ..scarf. was / were red. `✓`

On Wednesday, it was _____ . My _____ was /were green.

On Thursday, _____ yellow.

On Friday, _____ purple.

On Saturday, _____ orange.

On Sunday, _____ black.

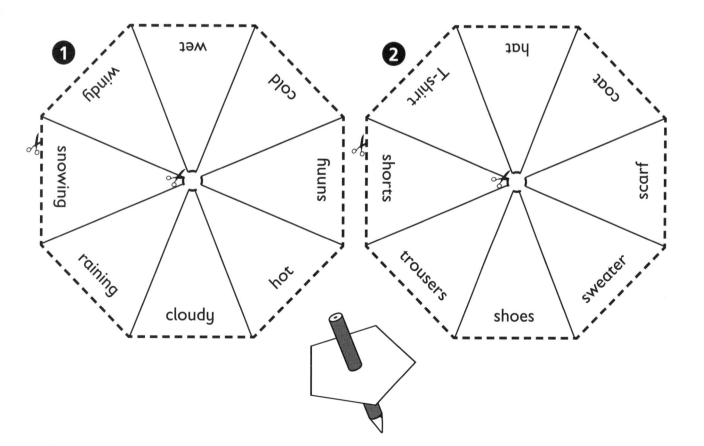

Extension worksheet 2

⑱ Think and write.

```
        6
        |
     5  r
  2  .  i  . . . . . . .
        g
        h    3 . . . .        4 . . 8 .
        t
```

Across →

1 How many people are in picture 3?

2 Lock and Key go to the _____ to ask Robin Motors some questions.

3 What is the name of the street Lock is talking about?

4 What is the name of Robin Motors' brother?

Down ↓

5 In picture 6, Key says he was _____ .

6 What day does Lock ask Robin Motors about?

7 What's the weather like in picture 2? It's _____ .

8 Lock and Key haven't got a _____ .

Song worksheet

 Listen and do. Sing.

BAT ...hat..., GOAT _____ , sweater
   and scarf,

It was cold and windy in the DARK _____ ,
   cold and windy …

It was DAY _____ and cloudy,

There wasn't any ONE _____ ,

There weren't many children, it wasn't much
   SUN _____ .

BAT _____ , GOAT _____ , sweater
   and scarf,

It was cold and windy in the DARK _____ ,
   cold and windy …

There wasn't a rainbow,

There wasn't any GO _____ ,

Grandpa and EYE _____ were ready
   to SNOW _____ .

BAT _____ , GOAT _____ , sweater
   and scarf,

It was cold and windy in the DARK _____ ,
   cold and windy …

JACK _____ at home,

It was much better,

With a NOT _____ drink, and my big BED
   _____ sweater.

BAT _____ , GOAT _____ , sweater
   and scarf,

It was cold and windy in the DARK _____ ,
   cold and windy …

BAT	hat

Unit 8 Topic worksheet

 Read and make.

The harp is a string instrument. The person who plays a harp is called a harper or a harpist.

My harp

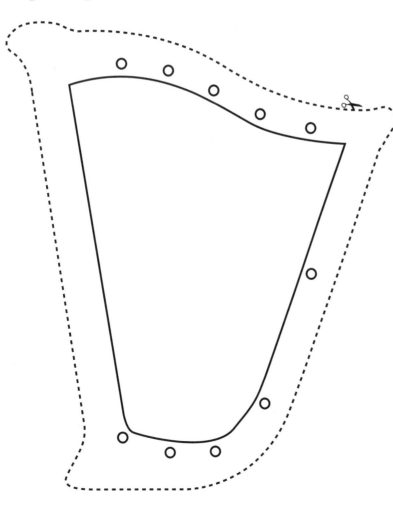

A harp looks like a big triangle. Some harps are small, but some are very big. A harp can weigh **36** kilograms and it can be **1.8** metres tall. Are you bigger or smaller than a big harp?

Harps are important in Wales and Ireland. Can you see Wales and Ireland on the map? The music from Wales and Ireland is called Celtic music.

In Ireland, the harp is on some flags and on the one euro coin. Try to find a euro coin from Ireland to show to your teacher and friends.

Festivals

Halloween

- The following cultural notes describe both the origins and the current traditions of this festival. Explain as much as you feel is relevant to the class.

- Halloween is celebrated on 31 October in the United Kingdom, the United States, Canada, Australia, New Zealand and many other countries around the world. It is not a public holiday in the United Kingdom. However, it is a very important celebration for children. The word 'Halloween' originally came from *All Hallow's Eve*, which means the evening before the Day of the Holy Ones or All Saints Day, 1 November. The tradition goes that on this night, spirits, ghosts and witches wander the earth. People used to make lanterns out of pumpkins and place them in the window to scare away these frightening creatures.

- Nowadays, on the night of Halloween, children get dressed up as witches, ghosts, vampires and other scary monsters and have a fancy dress party. Items that are traditionally associated with Halloween are pumpkin lanterns, bats, spiders and black cats. Children often play a traditional game called apple bobbing. They have to bite an apple that is floating in water or hanging on a string. Typical party food is cakes and pizza decorated with horrible faces!

- At Halloween, children love to play *Trick or Treat*. They knock on neighbours' doors and ask *Trick or Treat?* If the neighbour chooses a treat he/she must offer the children sweets or chocolate. If not, the children will play a naughty trick, like using a water pistol! It's always a good idea to have treats ready for visitors at Halloween!

Halloween worksheet I

- Pupils read the sentences about bats and decide whether they are true or false. Pupils work in groups. They compare their answers and decide on a group answer. Give marks to each group for correct answers.

- Pupils need scissors and elastic. NB. It is a good idea to photocopy the template onto card. Alternatively it could be glued or stapled to a strip of card.

- Pupils colour the bat black and cut along the dotted line to make a mask. They then thread elastic through the holes.

Key: 1 F, 2 F, 3 F (bats and mice belong to different families), 4 T, 5 F (they have one every year), 6 F (70 percent are insectivores; the rest eat pollen and fruit. The vampire bats of Latin America eat blood – you can decide whether or not to tell the pupils about the blood!).

- *Optional follow-up activity:* Pupils all wear their masks and stand in a row. One pupil takes off his/her mask and stands apart. Point to a masked pupil and ask *Who is it?* The pupil without the mask names him/her.

Halloween worksheet 2

- Pupils look at the spell, count how many of each item the witch has and then write how many she needs to buy. They invent a reason for the spell.

Key: 2 frogs, 3 lizards, 2 spiders, 5 eyes, 4 snakes. Suggested reasons for spell: To make her cat green. To be young and beautiful.

- *Optional follow-up activity:* Pupils invent new spells and what they are for. They can draw the ingredients.

Christmas

- The following cultural notes describe both the origins and the current traditions of this festival. Explain as much as you feel is relevant to the class.

- Christmas Day is celebrated in countries around the world on 25 December, to commemorate the birth of Jesus. In the weeks before Christmas, people decorate a Christmas tree with ornaments. They usually put a star on the top to remind them of the story of the birth of Jesus and the Three Wise Men. People also like to send each other Christmas cards with typical Christmas scenes and a Christmas message. Younger children write a letter to Father Christmas, or Santa Claus as he is sometimes called, to tell him what they would like for Christmas. On Christmas Eve, 24 December, they hang a Christmas stocking at the end of their bed or by the fireplace, if they have one. Traditionally Father Christmas arrives in his sleigh pulled by reindeer. He flies through the air, lands on the roofs of children's houses and delivers the presents by climbing down the chimneys with a huge sack of presents!

- On Christmas Day, families come together to eat a traditional midday meal. This consists of roast turkey, with vegetables. Dessert is a rich fruit pudding served with a brandy sauce that is set alight! The table is decorated with candles and brightly coloured crackers. Everyone pulls the crackers, which make a loud bang. Children love to look inside the crackers to find a colourful paper Christmas hat, a small toy and a Christmas joke.

Christmas worksheet 1

- Pupils need brown, grey and red pens or pencils, scissors and glue.

- Pupils follow the instructions to make a Christmas robin decoration.

- *Optional follow-up activity:* Tell the class the legend about the robin's red breast. In the old days, robins were only brown and white. When Jesus was born, he was very cold. The fire was going out and the Virgin Mary was too tired to blow on the embers. She asked the oxen but they said no. She asked the ass but he said no. A robin came into the stable. The robin started flapping his wings to make some heat for the baby. A spark from the fire landed on the robin's breast and turned it red. Jesus was warm so the Virgin Mary said that, from then on, robins could always have red breasts.

Ask the pupils if they know any legends about other animals.

Christmas worksheet 2

- Pupils need three cardboard toilet roll cylinders, crepe or tissue paper, thread, stickers, sticky tape and scissors.

- Pupils follow the instructions to make a Christmas cracker. Help them to understand the joke ('rain, dear' sounds like 'reindeer', the animal that pulls Father Christmas's sleigh. 'Dear' is a term of endearment often used by older people).

- *Optional follow-up activity:* Pupils tell Christmas jokes. Help them to say them in English. Suggestions for Christmas jokes: What falls in the North Pole, but never gets hurt? Snow! What do monkeys sing at Christmas? Jungle Bells!

Easter

- The following cultural notes describe both the origins and current traditions of this festival. Explain as much as you feel is relevant to the class.

  - Easter celebrates the resurrection of Jesus in the Christian religion. Easter Sunday always falls in spring. However, the date is fixed according to the lunar calendar and therefore differs slightly every year. In the weeks before Easter, people send Easter cards to friends and family, and they buy chocolate Easter eggs and Easter bunnies for the children. Many children like to boil real eggs and then paint them with bright colours. Children often have egg rolling competitions or hold Easter egg hunts with the colourful eggs. Easter baskets are associated with Easter. People fill them with Easter eggs and spring flowers to decorate their houses.

  - In the United Kingdom, people like to eat hot cross buns with lots of butter at Easter. These pastries are marked with a cross, which represents the Christian cross, and were traditionally eaten during Lent. In the Middle Ages, bakers would sell these buns in the streets. Of course, Easter is a time when a lot of people like to go to church. It is an important time of the year and Good Friday and Easter Monday are public holidays.

Easter worksheet 1

- Pupils need green and yellow pens or pencils, scissors and a yellow egg carton section. NB. It is a good idea to photocopy the template onto card and to enlarge it, if possible.
- Pupils follow the instructions to make an Easter card.
- *Optional follow-up activity:* Tell the pupils that the daffodil is the national flower of Wales. Show them where Wales is on a map. You could use the map on page 70.

Easter worksheet 2

- Pupils need an egg, felt tips, some kitchen roll and cotton wool, mustard and cress seeds. NB. If appropriate, send a note to parents so that pupils crack, wash and dry the egg at home.
- Pupils follow the instructions to make an egg head.
- *Optional follow-up activity:* Pupils keep a diary about the growth of the seeds, or 'hair'. Help them with this. For example:
Week/day 1. I water the seeds.
Week/day 2. The seeds are growing.
Week/day 3. I can see the plant. It looks like hair!

Halloween worksheet 1

Read and think. Tick true (T) or False (F).

1 Bats can't see.   T ☐   F ✓

2 Bats can't hear.   T ☐   F ☐

3 Bats are flying mice.   T ☐   F ☐

4 Bats can live more
   than 20 years.   T ☐   F ☐

5 Mother bats usually
   have five babies
   every year.   T ☐   F ☐

6 Thirty percent of
   bats eat insects.   T ☐   F ☐

Make a bat mask.

Halloween worksheet 2

Count and write.

Halloween spell

Four frogs   Seven eyes

Six lizards   Nine snakes

Eight spiders

What does the witch need to buy
for her spell? She needs to buy

Two frogs   _____ eyes   What is the spell for?

_____ lizards   _____ snakes   To _____

_____ spiders   _____ .

© Cambridge University Press 2015   Kid's Box Teacher's Resource Book 3

Christmas worksheet 1

 Read and make.

A Christmas decoration

- Colour the robins.
- Cut along the dotted lines.
- Glue the two halves together, inserting a straw between the two halves.
- Fold the top of the wings and glue them to the robin.

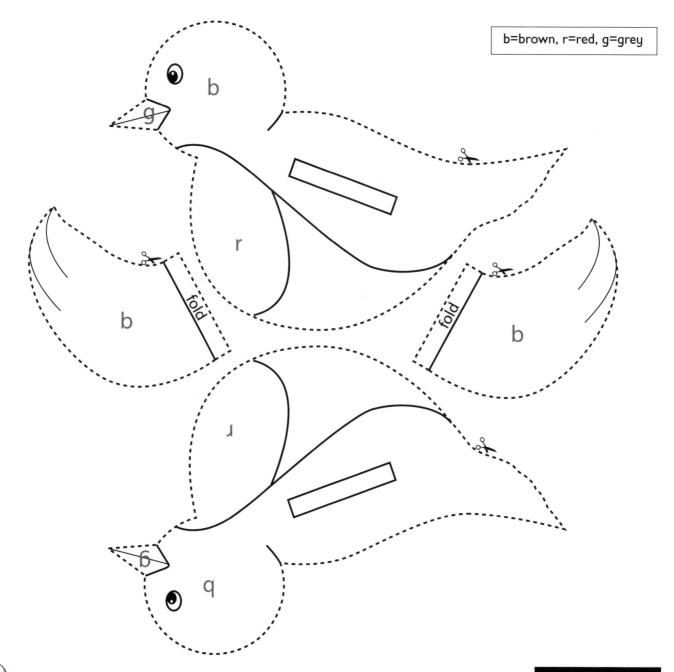

b=brown, r=red, g=grey

Kid's Box Teacher's Resource Book 3   © Cambridge University Press 2015

Christmas worksheet 2

 Read and make.

A Christmas cracker

- Make a paper hat with crepe or tissue paper.
- Cut out the joke.
- Put the hat and the joke inside a cardboard cylinder.
- Place another cylinder on each side of this one.
- Cut a piece of crepe or tissue paper 40cm x 20cm.
- Roll the crepe or tissue paper around the three cylinders.
- Tie thread between the cylinders.
- Take out the two end cylinders.
- Decorate the cracker with stickers.
- Pull it!

HAPPY CHRISTMAS!

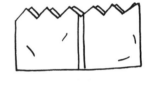

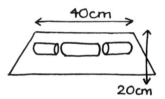

Father Christmas: *What's the weather like?*
Mother Christmas: *It looks like rain, dear.*

Easter worksheet 1

 Read and make.

An Easter card

- Colour the grass, stem and leaves green.
- Colour the daffodil flower yellow.
- Cut along the dotted line, then fold the card in half.
- Cut out a yellow egg carton section. If it's another colour, colour it yellow.
- Stick it in the middle of the flower to make the trumpet.

fold

HAPPY EASTER!

Easter worksheet 2

Read and make.

At Easter, people give Easter eggs. You can make one with hair!

- Crack an egg near the top.
- Wash it and dry it.
- Use felt tips to draw a face.
- Put wet kitchen roll and then wet cotton wool in the egg.
- Put mustard and cress seeds on the cotton wool.
- Put the egg in a warm light place.
- Wait a few days or a week. Keep the cotton wool damp.
- The seeds will grow and look like hair!

© Cambridge University Press 2015   Kid's Box Teacher's Resource Book 3

Word cards: alphabet

a	b	c	d
e	f	g	h
i	j	k	l
m	n	o	p
q	r	s	t
u	v	w	x
y	z		

Kid's Box Teacher's Resource Book 3 Word cards © Cambridge University Press 2015 **PHOTOCOPIABLE**

Word cards: numbers

12	twelve	20	twenty
13	thirteen	30	thirty
14	fourteen	40	forty
15	fifteen	50	fifty
16	sixteen	60	sixty
17	seventeen	70	seventy
18	eighteen	80	eighty
19	nineteen	90	ninety

Word cards: Family matters

aunt

daughter

granddaughter

grandson

grandparents

son

uncle

Word cards: Home sweet home

stairs

basement

lift

balcony

village

flat

city

upstairs

downstairs

town

Word cards: A day in the life

get dressed

get undressed

get up

go to bed

have a shower

put on

take off

wake up

wash

seven o'clock

Kid's Box Teacher's Resource Book 3 Word cards   © Cambridge University Press 2015   **PHOTOCOPIABLE**

Word cards: In the city

bank

bus station

cinema

sports centre

supermarket

swimming pool

library

market

a temperature

a cold

a cough

a headache

a toothache

a stomach-ache

Kid's Box Teacher's Resource Book 3 Word cards © Cambridge University Press 2015 **PHOTOCOPIABLE**

Word cards: A day in the country

grass

picnic

leaf

field

plant

forest

river

lake

© Cambridge University Press 2015   Kid's Box Teacher's Resource Book 3 Word cards

Word cards: World of animals

bear

whale

panda

bat

lion

kangaroo

parrot

dolphin

shark

 Kid's Box Teacher's Resource Book 3 Word cards   © Cambridge University Press 2015   **PHOTOCOPIABLE**

Word cards: Weather report

cloudy

raining

snowing

sunny

wet

windy

hot

cold

Name: ....

Class: ....

 20 **Listen and draw lines. There is one example.**

Jack   Daisy   Jane   Fred

Vicky   Sally   Peter

2 **21 Listen and write. There is one example.**

MY FAMILY

Name: .... Vicky ....

1 How old? ....

2 How many brothers? ....

3 Sister's name: ....

4 Mum's age: ....

5 Colour of Dad's beard: ....

3 🔊 **22 What's Sam doing this week?**

Listen and draw a line from the day to the correct picture. There is one example.

Monday
Tuesday
Wednesday
Thursday
Friday
Saturday
Sunday

Kid's Box TRB 3   Test Units 1–4   p3 Listening   © Cambridge University Press 2015   **PHOTOCOPIABLE**

4 📻²³ **Listen and tick (✓) the box. There is one example.**

What present is Tom buying?

A ☐

B ✓

C ☐

1 How old is Peter on Saturday?

A ☐

B ☐

C ☐

2 Where are they going swimming?

A ☐

B ☐

C ☐

3 Which woman is Peter's mum?

A ☐   **B** ☐   **C** ☐

4 Which is Peter's house?

A ☐   **B** ☐   **C** ☐

5 What time is the tennis lesson?

A ☐   **B** ☐   **C** ☐

Kid's Box TRB 3   Test Units 1–4   p5 Listening   © Cambridge University Press 2015

5 🎧 **Listen and colour and write. There is one example.**

© Cambridge University Press 2015   p6 Listening   Test Units 1–4   Kid's Box TRB 3   **95** (**95**)

Test Units 1-4

Name: ....

Class: ....

1 Look and read. Choose the correct words and write them on the lines. There is one example.

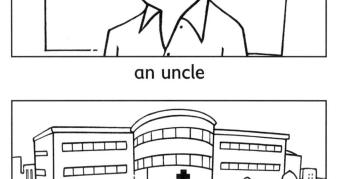

an uncle

a café

a hospital

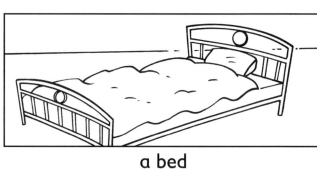

a bed

an aunt

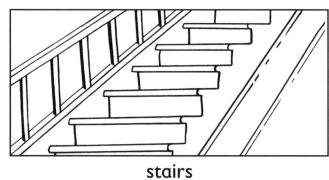

stairs

money

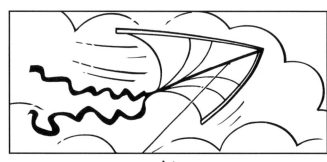

a kite

Kid's Box TRB 3 Test Units 1–4 p7 Reading & Writing © Cambridge University Press 2015 **PHOTOCOPIABLE**

Example

You can fly this in the park when it is windy.   .... *a kite* ....

Questions

1 You climb up and down these to go from one
floor to another.   ---------------------------

2 You can eat and drink here.   ---------------------------

3 This is where you sleep.   ---------------------------

4 Your mum or your dad's brother.   ---------------------------

5 You need this if you want to buy something.   ---------------------------

6 Some people must go here when they are
very ill.   ---------------------------

2 **Look and read. Write yes or no.**

Examples

The woman with the girl is wearing glasses.   ....yes............

The man who is making the sandwiches has a moustache.   ....no............

Questions

1 The girl is playing with a toy car.   --------------------------

2 There's a cat under the table.   --------------------------

3 The grandparents are playing a board game
with the boys.   --------------------------

4 A woman is putting ten candles on the cake.   --------------------------

5 There is orange juice for eight people.   --------------------------

6 The boys are sitting next to each other.   --------------------------

Read the text and choose the best answer.

Example

Jane: What are you doing, Paul?

Paul: (A) I'm buying fruit.

          B   I buy fruit.

          C   I can buy fruit.

Questions

1 Jane: What fruit do you like?

   Paul: A   Yes, please.

          B   Apples, bananas and oranges.

          C   Chocolate and sweets.

2 Jane: Can I have a banana?

Paul: A Of course, here you are.

B Yes, I have.

C Yes, it does.

3 Jane: I want to buy some flowers. Where are they?

Paul: A No, thank you.

B You have to buy flowers.

C There, next to the meat.

4 Jane: Where are you going now?

Paul: A Every day.

B By bus.

C I'm going home.

5 Jane: Can I come with you?

Paul: A You can come here.

B I can see you.

C Of course.

6 Jane: Look, there's the bus.

Paul: A Yes, let's run to catch it.

B And there's a lorry.

C In front of the hospital.

Read the story. Choose a word from the box. Write the correct word next to numbers 1–6. There is one example.

It's seven o'clock and Sally is in _____bed_____ . Her mum comes in

to wake her up. First, she has a shower and then she looks out of the

1 _____ . She's happy because she can see the

2 _____ . She puts on her **3** _____ and skirt

and goes downstairs for breakfast. At eight o'clock, she leaves the house

and **4** _____ to the bus stop.

'Oh no!' she says. 'Where is my **5** _____ ?'

She runs back to the house. Then she runs back to the bus stop.

The **6** _____ sees her and waits.

'I'm lucky!' she says.

Kid's Box TRB 3 Test Units 1–4 p13 Reading & Writing © Cambridge University Press 2015 **PHOTOCOPIABLE**

bed

piano

sun

walks

bus driver

T-shirt

window

schoolbag

farmer

7 **Now choose the best name for the story. Tick one box.**

Sally's busy afternoon ☐

Sally walks to school ☐

A day in the life ☐

© Cambridge University Press 2015 p14 Reading & Writing Test Units 1–4 Kid's Box TRB 3

5 Look at the pictures and read the story. Write some words to complete the sentences about the story. You can use 1, 2 or 3 words.

A day out

It is Saturday. Jack and Sue live in a village but today they are in the city with their parents. They travel by bus and get off at the bus station. The bus station is by the shops. First, they go to the shoe shop. Jack needs some shoes and his sister needs some boots. Then they go to the music shop because their mum and dad want to buy some CDs.

Examples

It is _____Saturday_____ .

The children and their parents live _____in a village_____ .

Questions

1 Today the family is _____ .

2 The first shop they go to is _____ .

3 They buy some boots for _____ .

4 Next, the parents buy _____ .

Then they are thirsty and hungry. They go to a café to have a drink and some food. Mum and Dad have sandwiches, but Jack and Sue want cake. 'Please can we have some cake?' asks Jack. 'We never have cake!' 'OK,' says Dad. 'You can have cake today.' Jack chooses lemon cake and Sue has carrot cake.

5 They eat and drink in _____ .

6 Jack asks Dad for _____ .

When they finish eating, they go to the sports centre. The sports centre is by the park. They watch some children playing football. The black team has three goals and the white team has two goals. It is hot and they have an ice cream in the park. Jack drops his ice cream on his shoes. Now they are dirty. 'It doesn't matter,' says his mum. 'You can wear your new shoes.'

7 The sports centre is next to ....

8 .... has more goals.

9 They have an ice cream because ....

10 Mum says Jack can wear his ....

Blank page

6 Read the text. Choose the right words and write them on the lines.

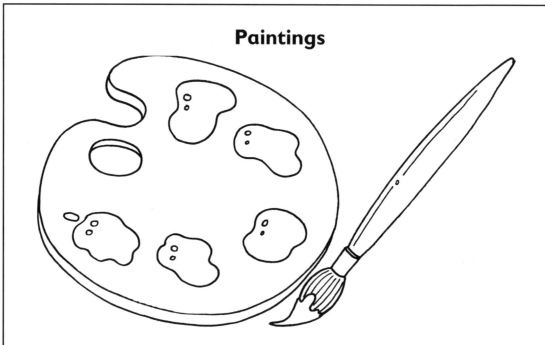

Paintings

Example	Artists _____ people who paint pictures. They paint all
1	kinds of pictures. Sometimes they paint people. _____
	pictures are called portraits. Sometimes they paint pictures
2	_____ the countryside. These paintings are called
	landscapes. Cave paintings are very old. They are of animals
3	and sometimes of people, but _____ of the countryside.
4	We can _____ see cave paintings of bears, lions and horses.
	In France, there is a picture of a horse on the wall of a cave.
5	It _____ 17,000 years old!

Kid's Box TRB 3 Test Units 1–4 p18 Reading & Writing © Cambridge University Press 2015 **PHOTOCOPIABLE**

Example	is	are	be
1	These	Them	They
2	for	from	of
3	sometimes	never	always
4	always	also	too
5	have	is	has

Find the Differences

Picture Story

Odd One Out

Kid's Box TRB 3   Test Units 1–4   p22 Speaking   © Cambridge University Press 2015   **PHOTOCOPIABLE**

Name: ....

Class: ....

  **Listen and draw lines. There is one example.**

Mary   Jack   Fred   Daisy

Sally   Vicky   Jim

2  **Listen and write. There is one example.**

THE WEATHER

Thursday: .... _wet_ ....

1 Cloudy: ....

2 What clothes? ....

3 Saturday: ....

4 Favourite weather: ....

5 Where snowing? ....

3 🔢 **Where was Tom last week?**

Listen and draw a line from the day to the correct picture. There is one example.

| Monday |
| Tuesday |
| Wednesday |
| Thursday |
| Friday |
| Saturday |
| Sunday |

 © Cambridge University Press 2015   p3 Listening   Test Units 5–8   Kid's Box TRB 3

28 **Listen and tick (✓) the box. There is one example.**

Which are Fred's favourite animals?

 A ☐

 B ✓

 C ☐

1 Which is the teacher?

 A ☐

 B ☐

 C ☐

2 Where are the children eating?

 A ☐

 B ☐

 C ☐

 Kid's Box TRB 3   Test Units 5–8   p4 Listening   © Cambridge University Press 2015   **PHOTOCOPIABLE**

3 Which is Fred's favourite?

 **A** ☐

 **B** ☐

 **C** ☐

4 What was the film about?

 **A** ☐

 **B** ☐

 **C** ☐

5 What time is it on the bus?

 **A** ☐

 **B** ☐

 **C** ☐

5 🔊 **Listen and colour and write. There is one example.**

Kid's Box TRB 3   Test Units 5–8   p6 Listening   © Cambridge University Press 2015   **PHOTOCOPIABLE**

Blank page

Name:

Class:

 Look and read. Choose the correct words and write them on the lines. There is one example.

a doctor   glasses

a picnic   shoes

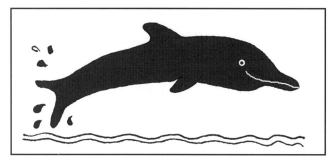

a dolphin   a rainbow

a forest   an elephant

Example

This person helps you when you are not well.   .... a doctor ....

Questions

1 You wear these when you can't see well.   ---------------------------

2 This is food you take to eat in the country.   ---------------------------

3 You see this when it rains and is sunny
at the same time.   ---------------------------

4 There are lots of trees here.   ---------------------------

5 This animal lives in the sea.   ---------------------------

6 You wear these on your feet.   ---------------------------

2 Look and read. Write yes or no.

Examples

There are four children.   ......yes......

There are two dads.   ......no......

Kid's Box TRB 3 Test Units 5–8 p9 Reading & Writing © Cambridge University Press 2015   **PHOTOCOPIABLE**

Questions

1 Both the women are reading.   ------------------------------

2 The girl with curly hair has got a stomach-ache.   ------------------------------

3 The boy on the floor is playing with a car.   ------------------------------

4 The boy with his dad is bigger than the boy
with his mum.   ------------------------------

5 The boy with his dad has a temperature.   ------------------------------

6 The girl with long straight hair is playing with
her brother.   ------------------------------

3 Read the text and choose the best answer.

Example

Jane: How are you?

Mary: A I'm in front of my house.

B I'm Mary.

C I'm fine.

Questions

1 Jane: What have you got there?

Mary: A Two big bags.

B Thank you.

C There is a car.

Kid's Box TRB 3 Test Units 5–8 p11 Reading & Writing © Cambridge University Press 2015

PHOTOCOPIABLE

21 Jane: Where are you going?

Mary: A Because I'm happy.

B To the beach.

C By car.

3 Jane: Is the weather nice there?

Mary: A Yes, it's hot and sunny.

B Yes, it's cold and it's snowing.

C No, I don't.

4 Jane: What's in the bags?

Mary: A On the floor.

B Jumpers and boots for sunny weather.

C Shorts and T-shirts for sunny weather.

5 Jane: Who are you going with?

Mary: A Yes, we are.

B I'm going tomorrow.

C My aunt and uncle.

6 Jane: How are you going?

Mary: A By car.

B Next week.

C The car is white.

4 **Read the story. Choose a word from the box.**
Write the correct word next to numbers 1–6.
There is one example.

My name is Vicky. I like photos. I've got a new .... _camera_ ....

This is my favourite photo. We are on holiday by a big **1** ....

My brother Tom is swimming, but the water's very cold! My dad is in

a small **2** .... He's **3** .... and he's showing us

an old **4** .... ! I like eating **5** .... but I don't like

eating boots! It was raining, but now it is sunny. You can see a

6 .... here.

camera

fish

bike

fishing

rainbow

boot

lake

boat

swimming

7 **Now choose the best name for the story. Tick one box.**

My dad likes fish ☐

A day by a lake ☐

A day by the sea ☐

5 Look at the pictures and read the story. Write some words to complete the sentences about the story. You can use 1, 2 or 3 words.

Vicky's computer

Mary and Vicky are sisters and John and Peter are their friends. Mary and John are nine, Peter is ten and Vicky is six. It is Wednesday. They are at the library working on the computers. Mary is looking at a picture of a lion. John is looking at a picture of a panda. Peter is looking at a picture of a parrot and a bat. Vicky can't see any animals.

Examples

The children are at _____the library_____ .

Mary has a _____sister_____ called Vicky.

Questions

1 Peter is ten. He is _____ than John.

2 John can see a picture of _____ .

3 _____ is looking at a picture of two animals.

4 Vicky can't _____ any animals on her computer.

Kid's Box TRB 3 Test Units 5–8 p15 Reading & Writing © Cambridge University Press 2015   **PHOTOCOPIABLE**

Peter can see a bear. The bear is eating a fish. John can see a dolphin in the sea. Mary can see a whale. The whale is bigger than the other animals. Vicky is sad. She hasn't got a picture on her computer.

5 The animal that Peter can see is eating _____.

6 Mary and John can see animals that live in the _____.

7 The animal that Mary can see is _____ than the other animals.

8 Vicky is _____ because she hasn't got a picture on her computer.

Four monkeys are in the library. Three of the computers are off.

Now Mary, Peter and John can't see any animals. Vicky's computer is on.

She can see a kangaroo with a baby. She is very happy.

9 The kangaroo's got a _____ .

10 Vicky is _____ than the other children.

Blank page

6 **Read the text. Choose the right words and write them on the lines.**

Dolphins

Example | Dolphins are not fish but they live ____in____ the sea. They are

mammals and their babies drink milk. They are clever like

1 chimpanzees. They can be under the water for three _____

2 four minutes. When they _____ sleeping, they stay under

the water but they come out of the water two times every

3 minute. They _____ wake up! They live together and they

help other dolphins who are weak or not well. Sometimes

4 _____ help people. They can see well and they can hear

5 better _____ people.

Example	in	on	under
1	and	or	into
2	is	was	are
3	don't	do	aren't
4	we	it	they
5	that	than	the

Find the Differences

Picture Story

Odd One Out

Test key and tapescript

Marks are not shown on the tests themselves to allow you the flexibility to mark in a way that suits your teaching situation. However, a suggested scheme is given below which you may wish to use. This scheme gives a total of 85 marks for each test. Note that all four skills carry equal weight in the Cambridge ESOL YLE Tests. There are two complete tests in this section.

Test Units 1-4 pp 90-112

Marking key

( ) = Acceptable extra words are placed in brackets
/ = A single slash is placed between acceptable alternative words within an answer
// = A double slash is placed between acceptable alternative complete answers

Page 1: Listening Part 1 (5 marks)

Key: Lines should be drawn between:
1 Jack and the boy on the bike with dark curly hair
2 Fred and the boy flying a kite
3 Vicky and the girl playing football
4 Daisy and the girl reading a book by the tree
5 Jane and the old woman asleep on the bench

TRACK 20

HEADING: *Look at the picture. Listen and look. There is one example.*
BOY: Hello. Are you with your parents?
GIRL: No, I'm with my Aunt Sally and my friends.
BOY: Where's your Aunt Sally?
GIRL: She's over there with her dog.
BOY: Oh yes! I like her dog.

HEADING: *Can you see the line? This is an example. Now you listen and draw lines.*
1
BOY: Who's the boy riding a bike?
GIRL: Which one?
BOY: The one with dark curly hair.
GIRL: Dark curly hair? He's called Jack.
2
GIRL: Look at Fred!
BOY: What's he doing?
GIRL: He's flying a kite.
BOY: Oh yes. It's a beautiful kite.
3
BOY: Who's the girl playing football?
GIRL: It's Vicky. She's with her brother.
BOY: They play well!
4
BOY: Who's the girl reading a book?
GIRL: Where?
BOY: By the tree.
GIRL: Oh, that's Daisy.

5
BOY: Look at the old woman.
GIRL: Oh! That's my grandma, Jane. Shh! She's sleeping.
BOY: She must be tired.
GIRL: Yes!

HEADING: *Now listen again.*
(The tapescript is repeated.)

Page 2: Listening Part 2 (5 marks)
Key: 1 8//eight, 2 2//two, 3 Jane, 4 37//thirty-seven, 5 black

TRACK 21

HEADING: *Listen and look. There is one example.*
WOMAN: Is this you?
GIRL: Yes, it's me.
WOMAN: What's your name?
GIRL: Vicky.
WOMAN: Can you spell that, please?
GIRL: Yes. V I C K Y.
WOMAN: Thank you.

HEADING: *Can you see the answer? Now you listen and write.*
1
WOMAN: How old are you, Vicky? Are you eight or nine?
GIRL: I'm eight.
WOMAN: Eight?
GIRL: That's right.
2
WOMAN: Can I ask you some questions about your family?
GIRL: OK.
WOMAN: First, how many brothers have you got?
GIRL: I've got two brothers.
WOMAN: What are their names?
GIRL: Peter and Paul.
3
WOMAN: Have you got a sister?
GIRL: Yes, she's nine.
WOMAN: What's her name?
GIRL: Jane. J A N E.
WOMAN: Jane? That's a nice name.
4
WOMAN: How old is your mum?
GIRL: She's 38. No, sorry. My dad's 38. My mum's 37.
WOMAN: Thirty-seven?
GIRL: Yes, that's right.
5
WOMAN: One more thing. Tell me about your dad.
GIRL: He's got a black beard and a moustache.
WOMAN: A black beard?
GIRL: Yes, and he likes playing football.
WOMAN: That's interesting. Thank you.

HEADING: *Now listen again.*
(The tapescript is repeated.)

Page 3: Listening Part 3 (5 marks)

Key: Friday   Sunday
        Thursday   Tuesday (example)
        Monday   Saturday

TRACK 22

HEADING: *Look at the pictures. What's Sam doing this week? Listen and look. There is one example.*
GIRL: How many books have you got?
BOY: Six.
GIRL: That's a lot of books.
BOY: Yes. I come to the library every Tuesday because I love reading.
GIRL: That's good.

HEADING: *Can you see the line from the word Tuesday? On Tuesday, Sam goes to the library. Now you listen and draw lines.*

1
GIRL: Hello, Sam. What are you doing?
BOY: I'm doing my homework.
GIRL: Do you always do your homework on Fridays?
BOY: Yes, because then I have more time to play at the weekend.
GIRL: That's a good idea.

2
GIRL: Oh, hello. Who are you with today?
BOY: The man with the beard and moustache is my grandpa and the woman with the short curly hair is my grandma.
GIRL: How often do you see your grandparents?
BOY: Every Thursday.
GIRL: That's nice.

3
GIRL: Sam, do you want to come to the cinema with me today?
BOY: I love the cinema but I play football every Monday.
GIRL: Who do you play with?
BOY: My friends.
GIRL: OK. Enjoy the match.

4
GIRL: Do you play football on Sundays, too?
BOY: No, on Sundays I visit my cousin. She lives in a flat in a big city. We watch the cars and people from the balcony.

5
GIRL: Oh, you're with your dad today.
BOY: Yes, that's right. I come to the market with my dad every Saturday.
GIRL: What's your dad buying?
BOY: Bananas. I love bananas.

HEADING: *Now listen again.*
(The tapescript is repeated.)

Pages 4 and 5: Listening Part 4 (5 marks)

Key: I C, 2 C, 3 B, 4 A, 5 B.

TRACK 23

HEADING: *Look at the pictures. Listen and look. There is one example.*
What present is Tom buying?
WOMAN: Hello, Tom. What are you doing here?
BOY: I'm buying a present for my friend, Peter. It's his birthday on Saturday.
WOMAN: Are you buying him a toy car?
BOY: No, he's got lots of cars and lots of lorries.
WOMAN: I know. You can buy him a kite.
BOY: That's a good idea.

HEADING: *Can you see the tick? Now you listen and tick the box.*

1 How old is Peter on Saturday?
WOMAN: How old is Peter?
BOY: He's eight now but he's nine on Saturday.
WOMAN: And how old are you?
BOY: I'm ten.

2 Where are they going swimming?
BOY: The party's at the swimming pool.
WOMAN: At the sports centre or at your school?
BOY: At the sports centre.
WOMAN: Where is it?
BOY: Next to the library.

3 Which woman is Peter's mum?
BOY: Look. That woman is Peter's mum.
WOMAN: Which woman?
BOY: The woman with long hair.
WOMAN: Is her hair straight or curly?
BOY: Curly.
WOMAN: Oh, yes.

4 Which is Peter's house?
WOMAN: Does Peter live near here?
BOY: Yes. He lives in a house by the park.
WOMAN: Is it big?
BOY: Yes, and it has a big garden.

5 What time is the tennis lesson?
BOY: What time is it?
WOMAN: It's four o'clock.
BOY: I must go. I've got a tennis lesson at five o'clock.
WOMAN: Have a nice time!
BOY: Thank you.

HEADING: *Now listen again.*
(The tapescript is repeated.)

Page 6: Listening Part 5 (5 marks)

Key: 1 Colour the doll's hair – brown, 2 Colour the star on the book – yellow, 3 Write SALLY below the portrait on the wall, 4 Colour the lamp next to the sofa – green, 5 Colour the clock on the wall – blue.

TRACK 24

HEADING: *Look at the picture. Listen and look. There is one example.*

WOMAN: Can you see the woman in the living room?
GIRL: There are two women in the picture.
WOMAN: Yes, but look at the old woman. She is the other woman's mum.
GIRL: Oh, yes.
WOMAN: Colour her hair grey.
GIRL: OK. I'm colouring it now.

HEADING: *Can you see the old woman's grey hair? This is an example. Now you listen and colour and write.*

1
GIRL: There's a little girl next to the sofa.
WOMAN: That's right. Her name's Jane.
GIRL: She's playing with a doll.
WOMAN: Do you want to colour the doll's hair?
GIRL: Yes, please. Can I colour it brown?
WOMAN: Yes, good idea!

2
WOMAN: Can you see the book on the table?
GIRL: Which one?
WOMAN: The one with a star.
GIRL: Oh, yes. Can I colour the star?
WOMAN: Yes, good idea!
GIRL: What colour?
WOMAN: Yellow.
GIRL: OK.

3
WOMAN: Can you see the painting on the wall?
GIRL: The portrait of a girl?
WOMAN: That's right. Can you write the name SALLY below it?
GIRL: OK. I'm writing that now.

4
WOMAN: Now, can you see the lamp?
GIRL: The one next to the sofa?
WOMAN: That's right.
GIRL: Can I colour it?
WOMAN: OK, what colour?
GIRL: Green is my favourite colour.
WOMAN: OK, that's a good colour for a lamp.

5
GIRL: I can see a clock on the wall.
WOMAN: You're right. Do you want to colour it?
GIRL: Yes, please. What colour can I use?
WOMAN: Blue is nice.
GIRL: OK. That's all.
WOMAN: Yes. Well done! The picture looks nice now.

HEADING: *Now listen again.*
(The tapescript is repeated.)

Pages 7 and 8: Reading & Writing Part 1 (6 marks)

Key: 1 stairs, 2 a café, 3 a bed, 4 an uncle, 5 money, 6 a hospital.

Pages 9 and 10: Reading & Writing Part 2 (6 marks)

Key: 1 no, 2 no, 3 yes, 4 no, 5 yes, 6 no.

Pages 11 and 12: Reading & Writing Part 3 (6 marks)

Key: 1 B, 2 A, 3 C, 4 C, 5 C, 6 A.

Pages 13 and 14: Reading & Writing Part 4 (7 marks)

Key: 1 window, 2 sun, 3 T-shirt, 4 walks, 5 (school) bag, 6 (bus) driver, 7 A day in the life.

Pages 15, 16 and 17: Reading & Writing Part 5 (10 marks)

Key: 1 in the city, 2 (the/a) shoe shop, 3 Sue/Jack's sister// the girl, 4 (some) CDs, 5 (a/the) café, 6 (a/some) cake, 7 the park, 8 The black team, 9 it is hot//they are hot, 10 new shoes.

Pages 18 and 19: Reading & Writing Part 6 (5 marks)

Key: 1 These, 2 of, 3 never, 4 also, 5 is.

Pages 20, 21 and 22: Speaking (20 marks)

Preparation
● Photocopy, colour and cut out the cards on pages 110–112.
● Mount them on card and laminate them, if possible, for future use.
● Prepare reinforcement or extension worksheets or other work for the rest of the class to do while you work with individual pupils on the Speaking test.

Procedure
● Ask the pupil how old he/she is.
● Ask the pupil to describe several differences between the two Find the Differences pictures, e.g. 'This is a doll but this is a robot.'
● Begin to tell the story prompted by the Picture Story pictures, e.g. 'Kim is shopping with her mum and dad. Kim is looking at a toy dog in a toy shop. She wants the dog, but her mum says, "No, Kim, not now. Let's go to the park." ' Ask the pupil to continue with the story.
● Ask the pupil to choose one picture in each of the four Odd One Out sets, and to explain why it is the odd one out in that set, e.g. 'These are all people, but this is a toy.'
● Ask questions about the pupil, e.g. 'How many brothers and sisters have you got?'

Test Units 5-8 pp 113-136

Marking key

( ) = Acceptable extra words are placed in brackets

/ = A single slash is placed between acceptable alternative words within an answer

// = A double slash is placed between acceptable alternative complete answers

Page 1: Listening Part 1 (5 marks)

Key: Lines should be drawn between:
1. Mary and the woman with a hat eating a sandwich.
2. Daisy and the girl looking at the flowers.
3. Vicky and the woman drinking juice.
4. Jack and the man eating cake.
5. Sally and the girl eating a banana.

TRACK 25

HEADING: *Look at the picture. Listen and look. There is one example.*

WOMAN: Hello. I can't see Fred. Where is he?

GIRL: He's over there by the river.

WOMAN: Oh! Is he fishing?

GIRL: Yes. That's right.

HEADING: *Can you see the line? This is an example. Now you listen and draw lines.*

1

WOMAN: Who's the woman eating a sandwich?

GIRL: The one with the hat on?

WOMAN: Yes.

GIRL: That's Mary.

WOMAN: Is she your mum?

GIRL: No, she's my aunt.

2

GIRL: Do you like flowers?

WOMAN: Yes. I love them.

GIRL: My sister is looking at flowers now.

WOMAN: What's her name?

GIRL: Daisy.

WOMAN: Daisy! Like the flowers!

3

WOMAN: Is your mum here, too?

GIRL: Yes, she's sitting with my aunt.

WOMAN: Is she the one drinking juice?

GIRL: Yes, she's very thirsty! Her name's Vicky.

4

WOMAN: I can see someone who likes cake a lot!

GIRL: Yes, that's my dad, Jack.

WOMAN: What's his favourite?

GIRL: Chocolate cake. He's eating that now.

5

WOMAN: There's a little girl sitting between your mum and dad.

GIRL: Yes, that's my sister, Sally.

WOMAN: She's eating a banana.

GIRL: Yes. She loves fruit.

HEADING: *Now listen again.*

(The tapescript is repeated.)

Page 2: Listening Part 2 (5 marks)

Key: 1 3//three, 2 (red) coat, 3 (it was) sunny, 4 snow// snowing, 5 (in/the) mountains.

TRACK 26

HEADING: *Listen and look. There is one example.*

MAN: What's this?

GIRL: It's my homework. I must write about the weather.

MAN: Put 'wet' next to Thursday because it was wet that day.

GIRL: That's right.

MAN: Well done.

HEADING: *Can you see the answer? Now you listen and write.*

1

MAN: What are you doing now?

GIRL: I must put the number of days it was cloudy in a week.

MAN: How many days was it cloudy?

GIRL: It was cloudy on three days.

2

MAN: Why are you writing 'coat'?

GIRL: Because we must write what clothes we wear when it's cold.

MAN: Do you like your coat?

GIRL: Yes, it's red and it's very warm.

3

MAN: Here it says 'Saturday'. It was sunny on Saturday.

GIRL: Yes, I'm writing 'sunny' now.

MAN: I like it when it's sunny.

GIRL: Me too!

4

MAN: Is sunny weather your favourite weather?

GIRL: Well, I love the sun but snow is better! I'm very happy when it snows.

MAN: It doesn't snow very often.

GIRL: I know!

5

MAN: Why does it say 'mountains' here?

GIRL: Because we must write where it was snowing on Sunday.

MAN: Do you like the mountains?

GIRL: Yes. I think they're great.

HEADING: *Now listen again.*

(The tapescript is repeated.)

Page 3: Listening Part 3 (5 marks)

Key: Saturday   Tuesday
Friday   Sunday
Monday (example)   Wednesday

TRACK 27

HEADING: *Look at the pictures. Where was Tom last week? Listen and look. There is one example.*

MAN: Hello, Tom. Where were you on Monday?
BOY: I was at the doctor's.
MAN: Are you ill?
BOY: Well, I was ill with a stomach-ache, but I'm OK now.
MAN: Oh, good!

HEADING: *Can you see the line from the word Monday? On Monday, Tom was at the doctor's. Now you listen and draw lines.*

1

BOY: Yesterday, I was at the cinema.
MAN: On Saturday?
BOY: Yes.
MAN: Who were you with?
BOY: I was with my friends.
MAN: Was the film good?
BOY: Yes, it was.

2

BOY: I was very happy on Wednesday.
MAN: Where were you?
BOY: I was in the countryside, by the river.
MAN: There are lots of ducks in the river.
BOY: Yes, and they were very hungry.

3

MAN: John says you often go to the sports centre.
BOY: That's right. We go every Friday to play football.
MAN: That's nice. Sport is good for you.

4

MAN: You weren't at the park on Sunday.
BOY: I know. It was wet. I don't like the rain.
MAN: But you weren't at home.
BOY: No, I wasn't. I was at the swimming pool.
MAN: So you don't like rain, but you like water!

5

MAN: It was sunny on Tuesday.
BOY: Yes, the weather was great.
MAN: Where were you?
BOY: I was in the mountains.
MAN: That's nice.

HEADING: *Now listen again.*
(The tapescript is repeated.)

Pages 4 and 5: Listening Part 4 (5 marks)

Key: 1 A, 2 B, 3 A, 4 C, 5 A.

TRACK 28

HEADING: *Look at the pictures. Listen and look. There is one example.*

Which are Fred's favourite animals?
WOMAN: Where were you yesterday, Fred?
BOY: I was at the zoo with my class.
WOMAN: There are some new giraffes at the zoo!
BOY: Yes, next to the elephants.
WOMAN: Do you like them?
BOY: Yes, but I like the monkeys more.

HEADING: *Can you see the tick? Now you listen and tick the box.*

1 Which is the teacher?
WOMAN: Was your teacher there with you?
BOY: Yes. She was very happy.
WOMAN: Is she old?
BOY: No, she's young. She's got long black hair.
WOMAN: Is it straight?
BOY: No, curly.

2 Where are the children eating?
BOY: Look at my photos. We're having a picnic.
WOMAN: I see. Was that in the zoo?
BOY: Yes. It was next to a cage.
WOMAN: Were you by the lions?
BOY: No, we were by the monkeys. It was very funny.

3 Which is Fred's favourite?
BOY: Look, this is a photo of me.
WOMAN: Oh, yes. What are you eating?
BOY: An ice cream.
WOMAN: Is it a chocolate ice cream?
BOY: No, banana.

4 What was the film about?
WOMAN: Were you at the zoo all day?
BOY: No. In the afternoon we went to the cinema to see a film about animals.
WOMAN: Was the film about elephants or lions?
BOY: No. It was about birds.

5 What time is it on the bus?
BOY: Look. This is us on the bus home. We're singing and laughing.
WOMAN: What time is it? Five o'clock?
BOY: No, seven o'clock.
WOMAN: It was a long day.
BOY: Yes, but it was a great day.

HEADING: *Now listen again.*
(The tapescript is repeated.)

Page 6: Listening Part 5 (5 marks)

Key: 1 Colour the flower in the girl's hand – orange,
2 Colour the big flower by the tree – yellow, 3 Colour the
blanket – blue, 4 Write PICNIC on the basket, 5 Colour
the flower by the blanket – red.

TRACK 29

HEADING: *Look at the picture. Listen and look. There is
one example.*
WOMAN: Can you see the girl?
GIRL: Yes, I can. She's having a picnic.
WOMAN: That's right.
GIRL: She's wearing shorts.
WOMAN: Yes. Colour her shorts black, please.
GIRL: OK.

HEADING: *Can you see the girl's black shorts? This is an
example. Now you listen and colour and write.*
1
GIRL: The girl's holding a flower.
WOMAN: That's right.
GIRL: Can I colour the flower orange?
WOMAN: That's a good idea.
2
WOMAN: Can you see the big flower?
GIRL: The one by the tree?
WOMAN: That's right.
GIRL: Shall I colour it?
WOMAN: Yes, colour the big flower yellow.
GIRL: Like the sun!
WOMAN: Yes.
3
WOMAN: The girl's sitting on a blanket.
GIRL: Yes. Do you want me to colour it?
WOMAN: OK. What colour?
GIRL: Can I colour the blanket blue?
WOMAN: Good idea.
4
WOMAN: Now, do you want to write something for me?
GIRL: What? A word?
WOMAN: That's right. Can you see the picnic?
GIRL: Yes. There's lots to eat and drink!
WOMAN: Yes, that's right. Can you write PICNIC on it?
 P I C N I C.
GIRL: OK. I'm writing that now.
WOMAN: Thank you.
5
GIRL: Look. There's another flower by the blanket.
WOMAN: By the blanket? Oh, yes.
GIRL: It's a nice flower.
WOMAN: What colour do you want to colour it?
GIRL: Is red OK?
WOMAN: Fine. Well done.

HEADING: *Now listen again.*
(The tapescript is repeated.)

Pages 7 and 8: Reading & Writing Part 1 (6 marks)

Key: 1 glasses, 2 a picnic, 3 a rainbow, 4 a forest, 5 a dolphin, 6 shoes.

Pages 9 and 10: Reading & Writing Part 2 (6 marks)

Key: 1 no, 2 yes, 3 no, 4 yes, 5 yes, 6 no.

Pages 11 and 12: Reading & Writing Part 3 (6 marks)

Key: 1 A, 2 B, 3 A, 4 C, 5 C, 6 A.

Pages 13 and 14: Reading & Writing Part 4 (7 marks)

Key: 1 lake, 2 boat, 3 fishing, 4 boot, 5 fish, 6 rainbow, 7 A day by a lake.

Pages 15, 16 and 17: Reading & Writing Part 5 (10 marks)

Key: 1 older, 2 a panda, 3 Peter, 4 see, 5 a fish, 6 sea, 7 bigger, 8 sad, 9 baby, 10 happier.

Pages 18 and 19: Reading & Writing Part 6 (5 marks)

Key: 1 or, 2 are, 3 don't, 4 they, 5 than.

Pages 20, 21 and 22: Speaking (20 marks)

Preparation
- Photocopy, colour and cut out the cards on pages 134–136.
- Mount them on card and laminate them, if possible, for future use.
- Prepare reinforcement or extension worksheets or other work for the rest of the class to do while you work with individual pupils on the Speaking test.

Procedure
- Ask the pupil how old he/she is.
- Ask the pupil to describe several differences between the two Find the Differences pictures, e.g. 'This is a hippo but this is a crocodile.'
- Begin to tell the story prompted by the Picture Story pictures, e.g. 'Mary is watching the weather report on television because she is going on holiday. She is sad because it is raining.' Ask the pupil to continue with the story.
- Ask the pupil to choose one picture in each of the four Odd One Out sets, and to explain why it is the odd one out in that set, e.g. 'These are all parts of the body but these are clothes.'
- Ask questions about the pupil, e.g. 'Where do you go on holiday?'

Diploma

This is to certify that

....

....

has completed

Level 3 of KID'S BOX

School ....

Teacher ....

Date ....

Thanks and acknowledgements

The authors would like to express their warmest thanks to Liane Grainger and Christine Barton for their encouragement, efficiency and editing skills. They would also like to thank Melanie Sharp for the beautiful artwork.

Kathryn Escribano also wishes to thank the staff and children at the CP Narciso Alonso Cortés, Valladolid (Spain) on whom the ideas have been tried and tested. Finally, she would like to acknowledge the patience and understanding of her family and friends from whom time was taken to write this book.

The authors and publishers are grateful to the following illustrators:

Melanie Sharp, c/o Sylvie Poggio; Gary Swift; Lisa Williams, c/o Sylvie Poggio; Emily Skinner, c/o Graham-Cameron Illustration; Lisa Smith, c/o Sylvie Poggio; Chris Garbutt, c/o Arena; Kelly Kennedy, c/o Sylvie Poggio

The publishers are grateful to the following for permission to reproduce photographic material:

Andrew Buckin / Shutterstock p.79 (pens); blickwinkel / Alamy p.79 (seeds); Colin Woodbridge / Alamy p.77 (toilet roll); Dianka Pyzhova / Shutterstock p.77 (Christmas trees); Digital Vision / Alamy p.77 (Sellotape); EML / Shutterstock p.79 (kitchen roll); Idamini / Alamy p.14 (Manx cat); Image Source / Corbis p.79 (cotton wool); Image Source Pink / Alamy p.77 (scissors); ImageState / Alamy p.70 (euro coin); Lebrecht Music and Arts Photo Library / Alamy p.70 (harp); Mau Horng / Shutterstock p.79 (egg); NDP / Alamy p.77 (tissue paper)

The publishers are grateful to the following contributors:

Pentacorbig: concept design, cover design, book design and page make-up
Wild Apple Design: second edition cover design and page make-up
John Green and Tim Woolf, TEFL Audio: audio recordings
Songs written and produced by Robert Lee, Dib Dib Dub Studios

Track listing

1 Introduction
2 Hello! Page 12.
3 Hello! Page 13.
4 Unit 1. Page 19.
5 Unit 1. Page 20.
6 Unit 2. Page 26.
7 Unit 2. Page 27.
8 Unit 3. Page 33.
9 Unit 3. Page 34.
10 Unit 4. Page 40.
11 Unit 4. Page 41.
12 Unit 5. Page 47.
13 Unit 5. Page 48.
14 Unit 6. Page 54.
15 Unit 6. Page 55.

16 Unit 7. Page 61.
17 Unit 7. Page 62.
18 Unit 8. Page 68.
19 Unit 8. Page 69.
20 Test. Units 1–4. Page 90. Listening 1.
21 Test. Units 1–4. Page 91. Listening 2.
22 Test. Units 1–4. Page 92. Listening 3.
23 Test. Units 1–4. Page 93–94. Listening 4.
24 Test. Units 1–4. Page 95. Listening 5.
25 Test. Units 5–8. Page 113. Listening 1.
26 Test. Units 5–8. Page 114. Listening 2.
27 Test. Units 5–8. Page 115. Listening 3.
28 Test. Units 5–8. Page 116–117. Listening 4.
29 Test. Units 5–8. Page 118. Listening 5.